From Awareness to Commitment in Public Health Campaigns

From Awareness to Commitment in Public Health Campaigns

The Awareness Myth

Myleea D. Hill and
Marceline Thompson-Hayes

LEXINGTON BOOKS
Lanham • Boulder • New York • London

Published by Lexington Books
An imprint of The Rowman & Littlefield Publishing Group, Inc.
4501 Forbes Boulevard, Suite 200, Lanham, Maryland 20706
www.rowman.com

Unit A, Whitacre Mews, 26-34 Stannary Street, London SE11 4AB

Copyright © 2017 by Lexington Books

All rights reserved. No part of this book may be reproduced in any form or by any electronic or mechanical means, including information storage and retrieval systems, without written permission from the publisher, except by a reviewer who may quote passages in a review.

British Library Cataloguing in Publication Information Available

Library of Congress Cataloging-in-Publication Data

Library of Congress Control Number: 2017944824

ISBN 978-1-4985-3329-4 (cloth : alk. paper)
ISBN 978-1-4985-3331-7 (pbk. : alk. paper)
ISBN 978-1-4985-3330-0 (electronic)

This book is dedicated to Eli Williams, Lucy Jo Hubbell, and in memory of Debbie Rothman . . . And all those grappling with health and healing . . . and to our mentors who knew this book would come, most especially Dr. David Cox, Dr. Linda Pledger, and Dr. Lynne M. Webb . . . and to our mothers: Sally Hill and Dr. Carol L. Thompson.

Contents

Foreword *Susan Jacobson and Lynne M. Webb*	ix
Acknowledgments	xvii
Unit 1	1
1 Overview and Introduction: Awareness is Everywhere	3
2 The Awareness Culture: The Rise of Ribbons and the Fall of Campaigns	13
3 Awareness as Events, Observations, and Amusement: An Analysis of Selected Health-Related Websites	27
Unit 2	43
4 The Awareness as Education Myth	45
5 The Awareness Is Enough Myth	53
6 The Awareness as Acceptance Myth	63
7 The Awareness Is Altruistic Myth	71
8 The Awareness Equals Health Myth	83
Unit 3	97
9 The Awareness Myth Model	99
10 The Development of the Commitment-Communication Model	111
Bibliography	125
Index	131

About the Authors   133

Foreword

Susan Jacobson and Lynne M. Webb

Every now and then, a book comes along that articulates a radical idea that is heresy to the field of communication and yet . . . the idea, once fully articulated, seems quite sensible and perhaps even obvious. *From Awareness to Commitment in Public Health Campaigns: The Awareness Myth* is such a book with such a message. Hill and Thompson-Hayes state the obvious: Health campaigns that focus on awareness fail to address more important goals. Awareness does not equal education, detection, prevention, or cure. In fact, as Hill and Thompson-Hayes argue, awareness is not even a meaningful first goal in an important chain of events but rather a small, necessary (but not sufficient) condition to a much larger end. Awareness is the equivalent of the "attention getter" in a public speech. If the speaker sat down after getting our attention, we would not consider the speech effective. However, corporate-supported awareness campaigns have spent billions of dollars, and collected billions more from donors, simply to "sit down" after gaining our awareness of various health malaises.

As Hill and Thompson-Hayes note, perhaps the ultimate awareness campaign is Breast Cancer Awareness Month. It is impossible to avoid the color pink in the United States during October. The association between breast cancer awareness and the color pink is perhaps the most successful public health campaign ever devised. But to what end? U.S. citizens see pink and think about breast cancer. Does this color association prompt women to obtain annual mammograms? Does it prompt men to ask the women in their lives if they have gotten mammograms? Does the money spent on pink ribbons actually fund breast cancer research to seek more effective treatment or to develop a cure for breast cancer? According to Hill and Thompson-Hayes's review of the literature, the answer is largely no, no, and absolutely no.

Hill and Thompson-Hayes would like their readers to ask why the funders of awareness campaigns continue spending money on pink ribbons when they could invest the money more wisely. They would like public relations professionals to aim for goals more meaningful than awareness in health campaigns, thus developing more impactful campaigns. They would like the general public to stop buying "pink" products unless the "donation" portion of their purchase is funding something beyond awareness. They would like communication scholars to develop and test health campaign models that move well beyond awareness as more important goals, indeed ultimately to the eradication of disease. We find their arguments compelling, their goals admirable, and their theoretical model heuristic. Below we identify the ideas we found particularly interesting from a scholarly perspective in this well-researched and well-written volume.

SCOPE OF THE VOLUME

In *From Awareness to Commitment in Public Health Campaigns: The Awareness Myth*, the authors examine the origins, causes, and implications of "awareness" campaigns, which they argue are more like "observances" than campaigns as "awareness does not necessarily translate into action and the end result of a campaign should, indeed, be action." The authors provide an extended critique of the impact of what they call "awareness culture," as outlined in the chapter titles: "The Awareness Is Enough Myth"; "The Awareness as Acceptance Myth"; "The Awareness as Education Myth"; "The Awareness Is Altruistic Myth"; "The Awareness Equals Health Myth." Although this is not the first book to question the value of awareness campaigns,[1] it deftly moves beyond critique to offer recommendations for alternative approaches to health campaigns and to provide a theoretical model for campaign communication.

Scholars will find very useful the critique of awareness campaigns and the communication model presented here. However, Hill and Thompson-Hayes's work is also valuable for public communication practitioners and activists who are seeking alternatives to the awareness campaign model. Additionally, students will find the writing accessible and the ideas interesting. We can readily imagine this book serving as a companion text in a course on health communication and in a course on campaigns.

MAJOR TENETS OF THE BOOK

Although the authors emphasize "ribbon" campaigns, such as the AIDS campaign in the early 1980s, the authors' dissection of awareness culture is generalizable to almost all health campaigns including, for example, framing rape prevention training for women as simply "awareness" of risks and risky situations (versus, e.g., martial arts training for women[2] as well as unmasking the myths of rape culture[3]). Hill and Thompson-Hayes challenge health communication and health care professionals to dig deeper to find a goal more important and interesting than simple awareness (e.g., raising funds to provide experimental or innovative treatment for large numbers of patients).

Ribbon campaigns are not created equal, of course. Wearing an AIDS ribbon in the early and mid-1980s was a political statement. In part, the widespread support for AIDS victims, as evidenced by the wearing of red ribbons, pressured government agencies such as the Centers for Disease Control and Prevention to divert funding to finding effective treatment for the deadly AIDS epidemic. The 2012 film *How to Survive a Plague* documents the success of the AIDS movement.

In contrast, a pink ribbon in support of breast cancer awareness makes no political statement and asserts no political pressure. In fact, ongoing emphasis on simple awareness can be interpreted to mean that we need not rush to find a cure until all potential victims know breast cancer exists and therefore can take the necessary preventative steps. The horrifying realization that many receivers *assume* awareness will automatically lead to prevention and that prevention will eradicate the disease—this is the horrifying legacy of awareness culture. Such an assumption flies in the face of the well-established fact that many women develop breast cancer despite preventative measures such as self-examination and regular mammograms.[4] In sum, the breast cancer awareness campaign may be actively preventing the necessary focus and funding needed to develop effective treatment and a cure for breast cancer.

"Awareness is not a goal" is perhaps the authors' most insightful critique of awareness culture. They link the goals of awareness campaigns to a misreading of Rogers's (2003) description of channels of communication in his Diffusion of Innovations theory: "'awareness' should not be an end goal of campaigns, but rather, like in diffusion, be an initial step leading to adoption—or action." The authors propose that "awareness" has taken the place of real, more difficult-to-achieve goals including education, prevention, behavior modification, funding for treatment, funding for translational (applied) research, and funding for basic scientific research. "The goal of our book, frankly, is to eliminate 'awareness' as a goal from public relations and public information health campaigns," the authors state. We agree. Communication scholars and professionals can do better, reach higher, achieve more by unleashing the power of effective communication for greater good.

What might such higher goals be for health campaigns? Hill and Thompson-Hayes offer multiple interesting options including education, testing, prevention, behavior modification (such as eating healthier), and social support for those diagnosed. Of course, the major goal of most health campaigns is to raise money, but to what end? Hill and Thompson-Hayes challenge professionals to consider raising money for higher goals including prevention, treatment, and research to identify cures and to end the disease itself. Any and all of these suggestions are superior to simple awareness.

To answer the question of how health campaigns developed such a myopic focus on awareness, Hill and Thompson-Hayes identify three historical developments that drive "awareness culture": inadequate government funding for research, corporate appetite for corporate cause marketing, and the development of the Internet.

Government funding for medical research has shrunk in the past decade. In inflation-adjusted dollars, U.S. federal funding of medical research declined 22 percent between 2003 and 2015.[5] The lack of government funding for research has motivated public health organizations to seek alternative methods for raising money. The authors describe the success of the ALS Ice Bucket Challenge, a grassroots Internet campaign that went viral and raised more than $100 million for research in one year. However, as Hill and Thompson-Hayes note, viral campaigns are difficult to replicate from year to year and from cause to cause. In contrast, "ribbon" campaigns are easily replicated; indeed, their ease and general applicability make them almost irresistibly attractive for an "easy win." Hill and Thompson-Hayes challenge communication professionals to move beyond the easy win to achieve more compelling and important goals such as funding innovative treatment and research to find the cure.

As Hill and Thompson-Hayes note, corporate cause marketing stepped in to fill the vacuum created by a lack of government research funding. But corporate cause marketing does not have raising money for research or finding a cure as its goal. The 2011 documentary *Pink Ribbons, Inc.*, about the business of breast cancer philanthropy, illustrated how some companies use pink ribbon–related marketing to increase sales while contributing only a small fraction of proceeds to the cause of breast cancer, and little or none to research.[6] Furthermore, by connecting products to charity causes, commercial interests may mask socially undesirable consequences of their enterprises through mechanisms like "pinkwashing," or the practice of improving corporate public image while manufacturing products that may be harmful.[7] Hill and Thompson-Hayes urge consumers to become discerning in their pink purchases and to question whether the donations will contribute to the cure or simply perpetuate awareness of the existence of the problem. Knowledge is power only when the knower takes action.

The Internet has fed awareness culture through what has become known as "slacktivism," or the act of "sharing" or "liking" or "retweeting" statements, articles, videos, or images depicting a problem, an issue, or a cause *instead of* engaging in real-life action to affirmatively address the problem. The authors describe the ALS Ice Bucket Challenge as more akin to promoting slacktivism than engaging an audience to commit to a cause. Another example, the 2014 hashtag #BringBackOurGirls, commemorated the kidnapping of more than 200 schoolgirls by Boko Haram in Nigeria; it went viral on the Internet but did nothing to actually bring any girls back home.[8]

Push-back efforts abound against "slacktivism." During October 2016, for example, many Facebook users posted memes saying "Wearing that pink in October does not provide mammograms for women, but Planned Parenthood does." Such push-back efforts tell us that the time for the book *From Awareness to Commitment in Public Health Campaigns: The Awareness Myth* is now.

AN ORIGINAL MODEL DEPICTING COMMUNICATION'S ROLE IN HEALTH OUTCOMES

Among the most impressive elements of the book is its culmination in a theoretical model that depicts the relationship between two sets of phenomena: (1) channels of communication (i.e., interpersonal communication, mass media, and social media) and (2) the development of individuals' participation in a health campaign (i.e., recognition/involvement, education/knowledge seeking, participation, and commitment). The model is notable for many reasons, but we would like to particularly praise its heuristic qualities, its success at illuminating the connection between communication and health outcomes, and its exploration of how participation develops, including putting awareness in its place.

The model depicts four elements as overlapping circles: recognition/involvement, education/knowledge seeking, participation, and commitment. These elements can be conceptualized as steps leading to the ultimate destination of commitment to a behavior (such as regular exercise) or a cause (such as raising money each year for cancer research). Alternatively, these elements can be conceptualized as multiple goals in a campaign that, ideally but not necessarily, overlap in such a way as to trigger one another. That is, awareness (recognition/involvement) is only one element in the chain of events that lead to an individual's commitment to healthy outcomes. Ideally, awareness overlaps with education/knowledge and participation, ultimately leading to commitment, but, of course, this is not always the case. In other words, awareness is not usefully an end in itself.

We see this model guiding future research for multiple reasons including its clear depiction of the interrelationships between the channels of communication. Indeed, many personal and public messages appear in multiple media and then are discussed face-to-face. How does such multicommunicating impact health outcomes? Are certain combinations more helpful than others? We also see future researchers testing and parceling the interrelationships between recognition/involvement, education/knowledge seeking, participation, and commitment. Future researchers may ask what factors lead to individuals' rapid development from recognition to commitment. Could it be characteristics of the illness itself such as its saliency, severity, or rarity?

LOOKING FORWARD AND THE POTENTIALLY USEFUL ROLE OF SOCIAL MEDIA IN HEALTH CAMPAIGNS

The authors have extensively mapped the implications of awareness culture as evidenced by the chapter headings they have chosen for this work. Their study of campaigns reveals how organizations communicate to the public, and paves the way for future research to investigate how different publics may communicate with health organizations or among each other.

Social media provide pathways for organizations to publicize their messages to networks of individuals, but also allow citizens to communicate among themselves about health-related issues, and thus social media provide a means for moving beyond slacktivism. For example, a loose coalition of organizations serving the needs of Stage IV metastatic breast cancer patients have adopted the slogan "Pink Is Not a Cure" as a sharp retort to the pink ribbon awareness campaigns launched every October by the Susan G. Komen Foundation, which spent only 20 percent of its funds on research in fiscal year 2015.[9] These organizations, which include METAvivor, MET-UP, Living Beyond Breast Cancer, and others, organize patients, doctors, and activists online to engage in direct action like "die-ins," letter-writing campaigns, boycotts, and in-person lobbying on Capitol Hill.[10]

Online communities dedicated to patient discussion of many medical conditions, from cancers to heart disease to arthritis, have emerged where patients may exchange information about hospitals and doctors, treatments and side effects. Many mommy blogs, for example, surround childhood concerns such as blogs for parents with autistic children.[11] Such communities provide social support, including informational support, that move well beyond awareness.[12] Social media figures prominently in the communication model the authors propose at the conclusion of this work. Their model may provide a road map for understanding these emerging online communities, and a way forward, a way beyond "awareness" to productive actions for scholars and practitioners of public campaigns.

In sum, we found this book a compelling and interesting read appropriate to many audiences. Because Hill and Thompson-Hayes base their claims on extensive research, their radical idea of abandoning awareness campaigns seems the logical next step toward both efficacy and morality in the public relations of health-related corporate causes. We believe *From Awareness to Commitment in Public Health Campaigns: The Awareness Myth* will convert every rational reader. We believe this highly accessible book will be well read, well cited, and well received inspiring many new studies and practices.

NOTES

1. See, for example, Samantha King, *Pink Ribbons, Inc.: Breast Cancer and the Politics of Philanthropy*. University of Minnesota Press, 2006.

2. Jocelyn A. Hollander. "Does Self-Defense Training Prevent Sexual Violence Against Women?" *Violence Against Women* 20 (2014): 252-69; Jocelyn A. Hollander. "The Importance of Self-defense Training for Sexual Violence Prevention." *Feminism & Psychology* 26 (2016): 207–26.

3. Elena L. Klaw, Kimberly A. Lonsway, Dianne R. Berg, Craig R. Waldo, Chevon Kothari, Christopher J. Mazurek, and Kurt E. Hegeman. "Challenging Rape Culture: Awareness, Emotion, and Action Through Campus Acquaintance Rape Education." *Women & Therapy* 28 (2005): 47-63.

4. See, for example: Miller, et. al. (2014) "Twenty five year follow-up for breast cancer incidence and mortality of the Canadian National Breast Screening Study: Randomized screening trial." *British Medical Journal*, February 11, 2014, 348:g366; Pace LE et al. "A Systematic Assessment of Benefits and Risks to Guide Breast Cancer Screening Decisions," *Journal of the American Medical Association*, 311(13):1327-1335.

5. Federation of American Societies for Experimental Biology (n.d.) "NIH Research Funding Trends." Available online: http://faseb.org/Science-Policy-and-Advocacy/Federal-Funding-Data/NIH-Research-Funding-Trends.aspx.

6. For example, the NFL's annual Pink October campaign sends proceeds to the American Cancer Society, but none of the funds are for research (Sinha, Smriti (2014) "The NFL's Pink October Does Not Raise Money for Cancer Research," Vice Sports, October 8. Available online: https://sports.vice.com/en_us/article/the-nfls-pink-october-does-not-raise-money-for-cancer-research.

7. For example, the energy firm Baker Hughes donated $100,000 to Komen for the right to sell bright pink drill bits to the fracking industry (Sirota, David. "Fracking's Disgraceful, Transparent New 'Pinkwashing,'" Salon.com, October 16, 2014. Available online: http://www.salon.com/2014/10/16/frackings_brazen_new_pinkwashing_con_partner/.

8. Sesay, Isha (2015) "#Bring Back Our Girls, One Year On: 'We Should All Feel Shame,'" CNN.com, April 14. Available online: http://www.cnn.com/2015/04/14/opinions/sesay-bring-back-our-girls-one-year-on/.

9. "Susan G. Komen Fiscal Year 2015 Annual Report" (2016). Available online: http://ww5.komen.org/uploadedFiles/_Komen/Content/About_Us/Financial_Reports/SGK-2015-Annual-Report-reader.pdf.

10. See, for example, the "Stage IV Stampede" campaign organized by METAVivor, MET-UP and others: Negley, Sonia (2016) "The Stage IV Stampede: Ensuring that Stage IV Gets More," METAVivor.org, Setptember 26. Available online: http://www.metavivor.org/blog/the-stage-iv-stampede-ensuring-that-stage-iv-gets-more/

11. Britney D. Lee and Lynne M. Webb. "Mommy Bloggers: Who They Are, What They Write About, and How They Are Shaping Motherhood in the 21st Century." *Gender in a transitional era: Changes and challenges*. Eds. Andrea R. Martinez and Lucy J. Miller, 41-57. Lanham, MD: Lexington Books, 2014.

12. Kevin B. Wright and Lynne M. Webb, Eds. *Computer Mediated Communication in Personal Relationships*. New York: Peter Lang Publishers, 2011.

Acknowledgments

The completion of this book would not have been possible without many people along the way. We appreciate and value their support and assistance. To Dr. Lynne M. Webb for "getting it!" and for her sound advice and time she spent talking to us about this project, and for just being who she is, a model of scholarship and professionalism with a gift for mentoring. To Susan Jacobson for agreeing to write the foreword and also for "getting it!" To Catherine Bahn for her help with research and our website and for patiently listening to us as we have talked about little else since this project began. To Emmanuel Omotayo Ogundigo for his help with the manuscript preparation, editing, and good cheer. To Christy Looney for being a sounding board and helping with our contacts. To Anne Russell-Skeene for her encouragement, advice, and for coining the phrase "sociological placebo." To Dr. Brad Rawlins for his encouragement and advice in the initial stages of our work. To our colleagues for showing an interest in our work and for their consistent encouragement. To our families and friends, who were supportive, encouraging, and never doubted we would get it done. And to so many more. And, of course, to the people who shared their stories with this. To all of you, we are truly grateful.

Unit 1

Chapter One

Overview and Introduction

Awareness is Everywhere

Ribbons are everywhere. In every color. Chances are you've been handed a pink ribbon. You've almost undoubtedly seen one. Or maybe you've worn a gold ribbon for childhood cancer. Or a red ribbon for AIDS. Ribbons have become a well-known if not all-encompassing symbol for awareness months. True, not every cause is represented by a ribbon. But, when you see a ribbon, there is almost undoubtedly a cause—often health related—hoping to "raise awareness." Raising awareness has become the default mission for health campaigns. In fact, according to the U.S. Department of Health and Human Services, there are more than two hundred National Health Observances, which are described as "special days, weeks, or months dedicated to raising awareness about important health topics" (1).

Awareness campaigns are rooted in The Women's Field Army, crea`ted in 1936 as part of an effort by the predecessor of the American Cancer Society (ACS). The "Khaki Brigade," as the women came to be called, went door-to-door sharing information to encourage women to get mammograms. The ACS credits The Women's Field Army with establishing it at the "forefront of voluntary health organizations" (6). Where the Khaki Brigade was distributing information provided by physicians, half a century later, cancer campaigns would take a more corporate turn. In 1985, the parent company of pharmaceutical giant AstraZeneca partnered with the ACS to establish National Breast Cancer Awareness Month in October. From the early years, the Sword of Hope was and remained the primary symbol of the ACS, but it was soon to have company from the ever-present and seemingly multiplying ribbons.

Later, though not specific to health campaigns, yellow ribbons became a symbol for supporting American soldiers. Then, AIDS activists noticed the popularity of yellow ribbons and designed red ribbons in support of those who were HIV positive. By the early 1990s, *New York Times* declared 1992 "The Year of the Ribbon" (Green 1992).

Perhaps the most prolific and popular ribbon, pink, started as a grassroots effort to call Congress to action. In 1991, Charlotte Haley handed out peach ribbons to grocery shoppers and mailed the ribbons to legislators to demand an increase in funding for breast cancer research. Cosmetic giants Estee Lauder and *Self Magazine* noticed Haley's effort and soon the companies branded her simple approach (despite Haley's disapproval based on her belief that they were commercializing the cause), changing the peach ribbon to pink and launching perhaps the most dominant and recognizable health campaign in the world (King 2006). By 1996, *New York Times* had declared breast cancer the "darling of corporate America" (Belkin 1996, para 35).

The advent of the Internet ushered in a new era of awareness raising, with a proliferation of ribbons connected to seemingly endless causes. The Internet allowed sustained, even continual "campaigns," perhaps better called "observances," as we will discuss in chapter 2. We use the term "awareness culture" to refer to a culture where awareness is seen as a panacea for all health problems so that simply being aware is thought to lead to positive health outcomes. *Awareness culture* is perpetuated through brandishing ribbons, participating in walks, and purchasing awareness products. Unfortunately, this only creates more awareness like an ever-increasing awareness bubble in which goals and objectives such as education, treatment, and research get lost in the bubble.

As the *awareness culture* developed, the approach went from door-to-door information about the benefits of mammograms to handing out ribbons at sporting events and sharing the colors of bras on Facebook. The Internet, and particularly social media network sites such as Facebook and YouTube, allowed for elements to go viral and reach millions of people, but that also brought questions of slacktivism. "Slacktivism," a term which merges the words "activism" and "slacker," is used to denote someone who provides a token display of support for a cause but is unwilling to devote time and effort in affecting real change (Kristofferson, White, and Peloza 2014).

Even as other causes were trying to emulate the success of breast cancer, the rise of the ribbons—particularly pink—was not without critics. In 2006, Samantha King published *Pink Ribbons, Inc.: Breast Cancer and the Politics of Philanthropy*. Robert Aronowitz followed in 2007 with *Unnatural History: Breast Cancer and American Society*. In 2012, Gayle Sulik criticized the breast cancer brand in *Pink Ribbon Blues: How Breast Cancer Culture Undermines Women's Health*. As stated by a 2014 *New York Magazine* article titled "Awareness Is Overrated," "We're living in the golden age of awareness-raising," but "the funny part about all this awareness raising is that it doesn't accomplish much" (Singal 2014, para 3).

Still, other causes continued to add ribbons and events in keeping with the *awareness culture* epitomized by breast cancer, such as Major League Baseball's partnership with Prostate Cancer Foundation for Father's Day awareness campaigns and fundraisers. Arguably the penultimate online awareness campaign was the 2014 Ice Bucket Challenge, which raised more than $100 million for the ALS Association (Wolff-Mann 2015). The campaign truly started as grassroots, with a few friends challenging each other to dump a bucket of ice water on their heads or make a donation to the ALS Association. The campaign went viral, with millions participating, but was not without controversy as some questioned the sustainability of the effort and how much participants actually knew about ALS, or if they were simply part of an online fad (Wolff-Mann 2015).

The *awareness culture* has continued to gain ground, even as some popular media voices have joined academics in questioning the impact of awareness campaigns and researchers have reported mixed results on their effectiveness. Our interest and formal study of *awareness culture* arose when personal circumstance matched a growing disenchantment with raising awareness.

One of the authors had developed a growing skepticism of awareness as an objective of health campaigns. She noticed that campaign organizers could seldom identify clear targets and measurements. She came to see "awareness objectives" as a "throwaway goal." Awareness objectives set the bar too low in that campaign planners could almost always claim increased awareness, but they set an unreachable bar, as there often were no measurable outcomes to provide evidence of the benefits of increased awareness. Awareness became personal to this researcher when her mother was diagnosed with breast cancer. The diagnosis came in early fall, with follow-up appointments and surgery coming during October—National Breast Cancer Awareness Month. The onslaught of pink everything—T-shirts, key chains, fundraisers, etc.—along with an endless variety of social media posts and games grew to be grating. Her mother confided that she and another friend, who had been diagnosed with breast cancer around the same time, were not fans of the proliferation of pink and didn't quite understand it. Breast Cancer Awareness Month? Aware of what? That there's cancer? Fundraisers made some sense, sure. But, what exactly was the benefit of football players wearing hot pink socks?

The other author, a mother of a child with autism, who had participated in awareness walks and purchased autism awareness products such as awareness ribbon keychains and magnets, observed that awareness as a public health campaign goal was not only limiting but could actually be counterproductive. For example, a person may repost an autism awareness image on

Instagram or Facebook without really doing anything to help autism treatment or research but still feel he or she actually helped the cause of autism. Moreover, a person could think he or she knows more about autism because he or she is aware of it but may not fully be able to empathize with people who struggle with autism in their lives. For example, one author had conversations with people who thought they knew more about autism than they really did because they were exposed to mass media awareness messages though they had little to no firsthand experience with people with autism. Such well-intentioned people can come across as uninformed, unhelpful, and not at all empathic. Still, awareness campaigns are pervasive and taken for granted as "good" for their respective causes.

When we came across an article entitled "Awareness . . . What a Bullsh*t Word" in the *Huffington Post,* we felt compelled to add our voice to the growing chorus. The article was written by Erin Santos (2013), the mother of a child who died of pediatric cancer, which challenged the efficacy of awareness as an end result of public awareness health campaigns. The Santos article went viral—liked on Facebook more than 16,000 times, shared more than 4,500 times, Tweeted forty-nine times, pinned on Pinterest twelve times, and e-mailed forty-five times.

We wanted to do what we could, as communication scholars, to help solve public health problems so we began our line of research on awareness in public health campaigns. To begin with, we thematically analyzed the comments to the Santos article and found three main themes (Hill and Thompson-Hayes 2014). First, responders indicated that action is what is necessary to combat childhood cancer and not just awareness. Second, posters stated that misinformation and "slacktivism" served as barriers to action. Several people noted that "likes" are not enough and the awareness generated in an awareness campaign may not be the type of information that is needed to create meaningful change. Third, posters indicated that personal relevance motivates involvement. In other words, respondents seemed to feel that unless someone is directly affected by a health problem, they will not get involved enough to create change.

Our next project (Hill and Thompson-Hayes 2015) was a case study of reactions to an article by Jennifer Wright (2010) that challenged popular Facebook games designed to raise breast cancer awareness titled "You Don't Need Facebook to Raise Awareness about Breast Cancer" (2010) published in *The Gloss*. We chose this as a case study because it represented a "critical case" to study awareness campaigns at a more grassroots level. Although not officially campaigns, these games appear on Facebook in order to generate breast cancer awareness. The first game, the bra color game, was featured on national news outlets such as *Good Morning America*. Other versions of the game have asked women to post a certain type of fruit to indicate their relationship status or where they would be traveling based on the month and year of their birth. The instructions for the games state that the games should be kept secret from men. These games, while popular, have their critics as can be seen from some of the posts to the Aarthun (2010) or Nieber (2010) articles. The most provocative of these games was the one in which women were asked where they put their purses when they first get home and were instructed to state it in the form of "I like it on the _____" in their Facebook status. Women's Facebook statuses read, for example, *I like it on the floor* or *I like it on the couch*. In response to this game, Wright (2010) wrote an article featuring a photo of a woman with a mastectomy stating that breast cancer is neither cute nor sexy but serious and deadly.

In our analysis of reactions to the Wright article, we found several themes. First, many respondents disagreed with Wright in what can be described as "backlash" against the author. She was told to "shut up" and to stop insulting everyone's intelligence by telling them how "unaware" they were. Second, many comments demonstrated support for Wright's arguments and even thanked her for stating that the games do not raise awareness. Third, we found that while some respondents found that the games were effective, many did not or viewed the games as only helping in the beginning of action or education. Taken together, our initial research offered reinforcement for the limitations of awareness and gave us some direction as to what factors can actually increase the effectiveness of health campaigns. A discussion of methodology for both published articles and primary research for this book can be found at www.theawarenessmyth.com.

The Awareness Myth addresses the prevalence of "Awareness Campaigns" that have burgeoned in the public relations arena, especially in the health and medical communication field. The premise of this book is that awareness is a misguided goal of public information campaigns. The core themes of the book are that (1) awareness campaigns have been oversaturated—and sometimes overcommercialized—to the point of being ineffective and perhaps counterproductive; (2) the scholarship surrounding awareness has been misunderstood, misapplied, and even ignored; and (3) educators and practitioners should move beyond awareness as an end goal in public health campaigns.

The Awareness Myth incorporates those arguments—that "awareness" is ineffective, over-rated, and counterproductive.

To defenders of the status quo of awareness campaigns, particularly to those including awareness as a goal of health communication campaigns, we argue that such default campaign goals are built on a misunderstanding and misapplication of communication theory, such as Rogers's *Diffusion of Innovations* (2003) and Grunig and Hunt's (1984) description of aware publics, and a neglect of research in other fields such as behavioral interventions. We further argue that despite its prominence in public health campaigns, "awareness" should not be an end goal of campaigns but rather, like in *Diffusion of Innovations*, be an initial step leading to adoption, action, and commitment.

A key issue is that while awareness might seem innocuous, there is some evidence that it actually leads to familiarity and a greater acceptance of the behavior in question—such as smoking. Another issue that makes this topic timely is that social media has allowed campaigns to largely bypass traditional news outlets in an attempt to disseminate information directly to the public, and our research has focused on reaction to those campaigns. We draw from Rogers's (2003) description of communication published in *Diffusion of Innovations* to build a case that media perhaps are effective at creating awareness but not at promoting adoption of an innovation. For example, the Ice Bucket Challenge generated ample publicity and even generated millions of dollars in fundraising for ALS in 2014, but two years later the sustainability of the phenomenon has been called into question (Nordrum 2015). Table 1.1 highlights a timeline of selected awareness health-related campaigns.

We use Rogers's *Diffusion of Innovations* theory as our primary theoretical framework. As noted by Littlejohn, Foss, and Oetzel (2017) although diffusions research is a long tradition, the most well-known and influential figure in this tradition is Everette Rogers. Rogers stated in the 2003 edition of *Diffusion of Innovations*, before his death in 2004, that there were more than 5,200 articles using Diffusion of Innovations theory at the rate of 120 articles per year. Given the reach of diffusion scholarship, an in-depth discussion of diffusion theory research is beyond our scope here and thus we refer readers to Rogers's preface (2003) for a broad overview of diffusions applications and research.

Again, although there were other scholars doing research in diffusion (Herbert Lionberger, e.g.), it is Everette Rogers's name that is almost exclusively associated with diffusion of innovations. Rogers drew from the ideas of Gabriel Tarde, whose "laws of imitation" stated that invention spreads through a social system by the process of imitation (Srivastava and Moreland 2012). Although Tarde focused on the diffusion process, his explanations of diffusion were based on outmoded psychological theory (Srivastava and Moreland 2012), so though Rogers was influenced by Tarde, Tarde's influence on diffusions occurs indirectly through the work of Rogers.

Rogers's diffusion tradition also was informed by the two-step flow of media influence, whereby the extent to which audiences were influenced by media was thought to be affected by interpersonal communication and opinion leaders in the social system (Srivastava and Moreland 2012). Rogers (2003) defined an innovation as an idea, practice, or object perceived as new by an individual or unit. Rogers (2003) stated that diffusion is the process by which an innovation is communicated via communication channels (i.e., interpersonal communication and mass media) over time among members of a social system. Rogers classified categories of adopters on the basis of their

Table 1.1. Timeline of Selected Health-Related Causes and Campaigns

Year	Event
1913	Ten doctors and five laypeople found the American Society for the Control of Cancer (ASCC) in New York City.
1924	American Heart Association founded.
1936	Volunteers in ASCC's Women's Field Army go door-to-door in an attempt to raise money and persuade women to have mammograms.
1945	ASCC reorganizes as American Cancer Society.
1965	Autism Society founded.
1970	Candlelighters forms as the first childhood cancer advocacy organization.
1971	President Nixon signs National Cancer Act of 1971—proclaims War on Cancer.
1983	President Ronald Reagan signs a proclamation designating November as National Alzheimer's Disease Awareness Month.
1985	ALS Association founded.
1992	*New York Times* declares "The Year of the Ribbon."
1993	Prostate Cancer Foundation founded.
1996	*New York Times* calls breast cancer cause "the darling of corporate America."
2005	Autism Speaks founded.
2007	Susan G. Komen Foundation trademarks "for the cure" and "pink running ribbon."
2008	Major League Baseball—Stand Up to Cancer.
2009	National Football League partners with ACS in Crucial Catch, promoting early screening for breast cancer. The website is nfl.com/pink.
2012	The U.S. Preventive Services Task Force (USPSTF) issues recommendations against prostate cancer screening.
2014	Ice Bucket Challenge raises more than $100 million for ALSA.
2016	President Obama announces in State of the Union address the Cancer Moonshot Task Force to be headed by Vice President Biden.

Table created by Hill and Thompson-Hayes.

innovativeness: innovators (venturesome people eager for new experiences), early adopters (usually opinion leaders within a social system), early majority (likely to have frequent interaction within the social system but not as opinion leaders), late majority (often adopt out of necessity or pressure), and laggards (traditional, more isolated in the social system).

In the first edition of *Diffusion of Innovations* (1962) Rogers, relying heavily on Ryan and Gross's (1943) work on the seed corn adoption process by Iowa farmers, stated that the stages in the innovation process were *awareness*, *interest*, *evaluation*, *trial*, and *adoption*. However, Rogers revised these stages in later editions of his book.

By the third edition (1982), the revised stages were (1) knowledge (occurs when individuals or decision-making units learn about an innovation), (2) persuasion (occurs when individuals or decision-making units develop favorable or unfavorable attitudes toward the innovation), (3) decision (occurs when individuals or decision-making unit engages in activities that lead to adoption or rejection of an innovation), (4) implementation (occurs when individuals or decision-making units use the innovation), and (5) confirmation (occurs when individuals or decision-making units reinforce or reverse their decisions). These are the stages present in the latest 2003 edition of the book.

Thus, it is important to consider how Rogers in the revised stages of the diffusion process (1982, 1995, 2003; Rogers and Shoemaker 1971) defined knowledge as incorporating awareness as awareness was not its own category and certainly was not the first stage. Rogers (2003) stated that there are three types of knowledge: awareness-knowledge (being exposed to the existence of an innovation), how-to knowledge (information regarding how to use an innovation properly), and principles-knowledge (principles underlying how an innovation works). He further stated that awareness-knowledge motivated individuals to seek out how-to and principles-knowledge. Thus, for Rogers', awareness is not an endpoint, nor a beginning, in the stages of adoption.

Despite this, some popular mass communication and public relations textbooks still use *awareness*, *interest*, *evaluation*, *trial*, and *adoption* in their discussions on diffusion (e.g., DeFleur and DeFleur 2016; Lattimore, Baskin, Heiman, Toth, and Van Leuven 2012). We do not understand why these authors did not include Rogers's later, revised stages which begin with knowledge and include awareness as part of a discussion on knowledge. Even if the adoption process did begin with awareness, it certainly doesn't end with awareness. In response to the argument that people must be exposed to awareness campaigns as a first step, we argue that with "awareness campaigns" there is never a next step as the goal of "awareness" was "achieved." Even if follow-up campaigns were to ensue, there was likely damage done in the awareness campaign. For example, since they were not actually taught anything but that a condition exists, people may actually have misconceptions about the condition. Furthermore, if people did participate in an awareness event or purchase a ribbon or awareness product, they may feel that their work is done with the cause. There may even be an effect of social loafing with people thinking that since so many people are talking about a cause, there is surely work being done improving it and so do not feel compelled to take action.

The goal of our book, frankly, is to eliminate "awareness" as a goal from public health campaigns. Given the widespread adoption of awareness as a goal and how steeped campaigns are in the *awareness culture*, however, the authors begin by proposing to "move the needle" beyond awareness to at least "how-to knowledge" and then spur adoption, action, and commitment. The Awareness Myth is rooted in the authors' original research that challenged awareness as a goal of campaigns. The book seeks to answer the question of how to go beyond the *awareness culture* to produce more effective health campaigns that will lead to eradicating disease and alleviating suffering. The book traces the development of the awareness campaigns and the awareness culture in Unit 1, presents common awareness myths in Unit 2, then follows with a presentation of the current Awareness Myth Model and proposes a new Commitment-Communication Model.

Our Commitment-Communication Model differs from previous models and theories of persuasion in health campaigns because it is dynamic and processual. One can enter into it from any point and movement can occur in any direction. The model depicts four factors affecting commitment, which refers to ongoing attempts to solve or alleviate a public health problem. The four factors in the model intersect.

The variables in our model are recognition involvement (i.e., degree to which individuals view a problem as needing to be addressed based on perceived level of personal salience and involvement with the problem), knowledge seeking/education (i.e., degree to which individuals seek knowledge about and become educated on a problem), and participation (i.e., degree to which people participate in specific activities, including communication activities, in order to alleviate the problem). At the center of the model is the variable commitment, surrounded by communication (i.e., the channels by which messages are communicated such as mass media, social media, and interpersonal communication), which is the process by which all variables interact.

We offer suggestions for public health campaign practitioners and directions for future research. For example, awareness should never be the endpoint of a public health campaign. Current mission statements should be rewritten so that awareness is not the ultimate goal of the campaign. Perhaps the goal is actually education, for example.

The Magic Bullet theory, now considered "quaint" and "simplistic" developed in retrospect, provides a comparison to the current fascination with awareness campaigns. We predict that in the coming decades as the effectiveness of health communication campaigns is studied more in depth and social media diffusion is better understood, awareness campaigns will be viewed as quaint and as simplistic as the Magic Bullet theory is now. Awareness will be seen as part of recognition—as a first step and not an end goal.

We hope to be part of this overall discussion leading to action, adoption, and commitment.

Chapter Two

The Awareness Culture

The Rise of Ribbons and the Fall of Campaigns

"Pink ribbons were strewn on the floor, and people were stepping on them as they left the gym...."

There can be no doubt that awareness campaigns have been highly visible across the country. What can be debated is the impact and effectiveness of awareness campaigns. In all the stories we heard in conversations and interviews about awareness, Elizabeth's symbolized the complexities and controversies now inherent in awareness campaigns and observances.

"They handed me a pink ribbon as I walked in," Elizabeth recalled. "Of course," she thought. "It's October, breast cancer awareness month." A sorority participating in a breast cancer awareness event was distributing pink ribbons to the crowd at a university volleyball game. Elizabeth remembers stepping around ribbons that people in front of her dropped on the floor after taking just a few steps. She put the ribbon in her purse; she didn't want to wear it, but she also found it disrespectful to simply discard it. During the game, breast cancer survivors were honored on the court and the announcer asked those in the crowd who had survived cancer to stand to be recognized. A polite, somewhat awkward applause followed. "Why are we clapping?" Elizabeth thought, slowly joining.

She shakes her head and draws a breath before sharing about leaving the gym after the end of the game. Walking out, so many ribbons were littered on the floor that she could not avoid stepping on them. Bright pink only a couple hours earlier, they were now dirty. A symbol of hope trashed. Elizabeth says she is not much on causes or walks or races. She never put the ribbon on at the game, but for some reason she could never bear to throw it away. She put it in a drawer, where it remains out of sight but not exactly out of mind.

Ever since the *New York Times* declared 1992 "The Year of the Ribbon" (Green), causes have been jockeying for position and competing for corporate dollars and even government funding. For two decades, the pink ribbon of Breast Cancer Awareness has stood out among the causes attempting to raise awareness—and donations. In a time when other causes and campaigns are vying for the exposure that the ubiquitous pink ribbon of breast cancer awareness has reached, the pink ribbon itself, while not exactly getting trampled, is the subject of a small backlash.

For example, in October of 2015, Gina Kolata of the *New York Times* wrote about "A Growing Disenchantment with October 'Pinkification'" (Kolata 2015). In 2012, Gayle Sulik, herself a breast cancer survivor, wrote a book titled *Pink Ribbon Blues: How Breast Cancer Culture Undermines Women's Health.* But even in the face of pockets of criticism, National Breast Cancer Awareness Month (NBCAM) in October remains a sea of pink with unmatched events and fundraisers. Our research leads us to believe that a reason why awareness months such as NBCAM continue to thrive is that the *awareness culture* they represent denotes a shift away from campaigns designed to advocate prevention or behavior change. Instead, the awareness observances feature a level of engagement that can be seen as social support for those involved or well-intentioned quasi-participation from those less affected. For example, an alumna called to tell us about a radio spot she heard during October 2016. She paraphrased the advertisement for a 5K run in support of breast cancer. "We're all aware of breast cancer," she remembers the spot saying, before going on to say the way to "do something" about it was to participate in the race.

Although breast cancer campaigns have the longest history and are the most visible currently, that is not to say that they have always been the most prominent of the health campaigns, particularly during the 1980s and early 90s. For example, the red ribbon in support of those with AIDS was once among the most well-known ribbons (http://www.disabled-world.com/disability/awareness/ribbons.php). Additionally and perhaps somewhat confusingly, Red Ribbon Week became a feature during the War on Drugs, encouraging young people to be drug free. In fact, Backer, Rogers, and Sopory published a book in 1992 titled *Designing Health Communication Campaigns: What Works?,* based on a grant from the Office of Substance Abuse Prevention. Backer, Rogers, and Sopory noted the number of health campaigns and the challenges of using health communication campaigns to change health behaviors and make meaningful interventions.

The early 1990s were a pivotal time in health campaigns. The rise of ribbons as documented in the *New York Times* piece "The Year of the Ribbon" (Green 1992) coincided with the book by Backer, Rogers, and Sopory (1992) on how best to implement effective campaigns. Ribbons were not part of their recommendations. Three main developments in the 1990s led to the *awareness culture,* which elevated observances at the expense of preventative health campaigns. Those developments were (1) inadequate government funding for research, (2) corporate cause marketing, and (3) the Internet. Taken together, these causes were a perfect storm. This chapter documents the findings and best practices of Backer, Rogers, and Sopory published in 1992 and then contrasts those findings and recommendations with the *New York Times's* article on ribbons in 1992 (Green) and *New York Times Magazine*'s 1996 feature on awareness raising and charity galas (Belkin). The description details how the theoretical models advocated by scholars such as Backer, Rogers, and Sopory were undermined by factors that were unforeseen in the early 1990s. Understanding how well-researched approaches gave way to symbols of awareness such as ribbons in health campaigns is important to build a foundation for our proposed Commitment-Communication Model.

BEST PRACTICES IN HEALTH CAMPAIGNS

Backer, Rogers, and Sopory (1992) presented two health communication campaigns, both developed in 1971, as exemplars. The campaigns were the Stanford Heart Disease Prevention Program, conducted in California, and the North Karelia Project, conducted in a province in Finland, which at the time had "the highest rates of cardiovascular disease in the world" (Backer, Rogers, and Sopory 1992, p. xiii). Both campaigns dealt with heart disease and also were examples of "mass media health campaigns" (Backer, Rogers, and Sopory, 1992, p. xiii). The authors noted the difficulty of preventative campaigns, which attempt to change behavior. Still, writing in 1992, they found factors that led to greater success in the recent decades of preventative campaigns:

> (1) They have been based on vigorous, empirically validated social science theories, such as social learning theory, social marketing, the health belief model, and the diffusion of innovations. (2) They have utilized formative evaluation research in order to improve the effectiveness of the communication campaign before it was launched or while it was under way. (3) In comparison with earlier campaigns, they have had more reasonable objectives (e.g., a goal of achieving a 3 percent reduction in the risk of heart disease in a four-year campaign) that are more likely to be reached. (Backer, Rogers, and Sopory 1992, xiv)

Citing the statistics on the number of deaths that could be "directly attributed to lifestyle and behavior factors" (Backer, Rogers, and Sopory 1992, 3) proposed health communication campaigns as a way to help address what they termed the societal problem. They noted that "television, radio, film, and print media are increasingly being used in creative ways to present health information and to stimulate awareness, attitude change, and behavior change" (Backer, Rogers, and Sopory 1992, 3) and that these campaigns often had interpersonal and community components as well. The authors presented a seven-point hierarchy of effects table that ranged from exposure and awareness to actual change and maintenance of change in the audience behavior. The authors also pointed out that preventative innovations were difficult to diffuse at a rapid pace because the reward is delayed, if achieved at all. In other words, it could be hard to convince someone to give up smoking or quit eating fatty foods to potentially lower a risk of heart disease in the future. Additionally, among those interviewed by Backer, Rogers, and Sopory (1992), there was disagreement on the use of hierarchy of effects models. While some said the hierarchical models were useful in structuring campaigns, others said the models did not take into account situations outside of controlled laboratory settings and that campaigns should instead incorporate sociological based theories such as Diffusion of Innovations and Social Learning Theory.

The North Karelia Project was presented by Backer, Rogers, and Sopory (1992) as a model of how an innovation can be introduced and gradually diffused over time. Citing the mass media as well as face-to-face community interactions, the authors concluded, "The effects of health promotion campaigns are cumulative, like a stalactite dripping, dripping, dripping. Slowly, the audience effects are built up" (Backer, Rogers, and Sopory 1992, 9). (The full details of the North Karelia Project are instructive but outside of the scope of this book. The authors highly recommend that those interested in the history and efficacy of health communication campaigns read Dan Buettner's article "The Finnish Town That Went on a Diet" in the April 7, 2015, issue of the *Atlantic*.)

Backer, Rogers, and Sopory (1992) were obviously building on Rogers's Diffusion of Innovation work as well as the work of other scholars in conducting their analysis of health communication campaigns. Furthermore, they conducted twenty-nine interviews of health communication campaign designers. The result was twenty-seven generalizations for campaign designs that served as a form of best practices. Generalizations relevant to today are discussed in Unit 3, particularly in relationship to mass media.

RIBBONS AND GALAS

The best practices recommended by Backer, Rogers, and Sopory (1992) didn't include recommendations for ribbons and observances, but ribbons were already becoming prominent as symbols for awareness causes. For example, the *New York Times* called 1992 the "Year of the Ribbon" (Green

1992). The ribbon of note was a red ribbon associated with AIDS. The organizers behind the AIDS ribbon had noticed the popularity of yellow ribbons that were still found following their peak years during the Gulf War. In particular, they noticed that the ribbon could have a variety of meanings and take a variety of shapes and styles. They hoped to build on the yellow ribbon model in showing support for a cause that at the time could be controversial. (The founders of Visual AIDS chose the color red, even though Mothers Against Drunk Driving was handing out red ribbons.) The red ribbons for AIDS became highly visible, which was both good and bad. "It's that very cheeriness, that second-prize-at-the-dog-show simplicity, that has made the ribbon successful—and threatened it as well" (Green 1992, para 10). Some considered the ribbon banal. Others, such as the executive director of Broadway Cares/Equity Fights AIDS, Rodger McFarlane, found it "an easy first step" (Green 1992, para 12) and a conversation starter. Still others saw it as a meaningless fashion statement for celebrities, some of whom wore jewel-encrusted ribbons to awards show.

The red ribbon proliferated despite the protest of AIDS educators. One said that the cheery red ribbon was missing the element of anger, and that sympathy would be powerless against a quarantine, which presumably could have developed in the absence of more effective and direct campaigns. For their part, supporters of the ribbon were mainly in agreement, according to the "Year of the Ribbon" article:

> "I never want this to seem like anything more than visibility," said Rodger McFarlane, executive director of Broadway Cares/Equity Fights AIDS. "The ribbon does not feed people or protect them from discrimination or provide leadership or a cure. But it is, at least, an easy first step."
> Mr. O'Connell of Visual AIDS goes further: "People want to say something, not necessarily with anger and confrontation all the time. This allows them. And even if it is only an easy first step, that's great with me. It won't be their last." (Green 1992, para 12-13)

However, the next step beyond wearing ribbons was never clearly articulated, and in fact the ribbons became commercialized against the wishes of the original red ribbon makers, who found beauty in the simplicity of homemade ribbons. Instead, ribbons began showing up on greeting cards and T-shirts. Whatever the intentions and legacy of the red AIDS ribbon, it helped establish the *awareness culture*. From AIDS ribbons to today, ribbons have come to symbolize awareness. Sometimes the ribbon has indeed been an "easy first step." However, too often the ribbon is also the *only* step and has not led to further participation, education, or commitment to behavior change.

By the mid-1990s, the *awareness culture* was beginning to take form, and it was not in the shape of the steady stream of information leading toward preventative campaigns and behavior change that Backer, Rogers, and Sopory (1992) had advocated. In 1996, *New York Times Magazine*, in an article titled "Charity Begins at . . . the Marketing Meeting, the Gala Event, the Product Tie-In," explained how breast cancer, and specifically the Komen Foundation, had become the "darling of corporate America" (Belkin 1996, para 36). Covering the Komen Foundation's gala in Dallas, Lisa Belkin described an "extravaganza" in which representatives of dozens of top-of-mind companies were recognized complete with military fanfare of walking under crossed swords as a color guard trumpet section played. Most of the representatives wore pink ribbons, and bowed their heads when they received medals around their necks:

> [It is] all part of what it takes to become the cause in the competitive world of causes; to remain the disease in an era when everyone, particularly during this season of giving, is trying to get attention for his or her disease. It is what it takes to elbow aside the previous hot crusade and find yourself being stared at and scrutinized by those who are blatantly waiting their turn to elbow you. Just yesterday, or so it seems, the ribbons were red and the cause was AIDS. Now, although money and empathy still flow to the AIDS cause, the pink team has pulled ahead in the philanthropic color war, and the cause is breast cancer. (Belkin 1996, para 5)

Belkin (1996) continued to explain how statistically breast cancer is an unlikely candidate to win the color ribbon war—it was not the leading cause of death, which was heart disease, or even the most lethal of cancers, which was lung cancer. Instead, the article stated, the breast cancer movement was about the fears of women:

> Heart disease and lung cancer—those bring fear of death, yes, but breast cancer carries an even weightier load. To women, it is not only about mortality, it is about intimacy, femininity, sexuality and sense of self. Since the single greatest risk factor for breast cancer is not family history or environment or behavior, but simply being female, it makes women feel as if they are under attack just because they are women. The new visibility of breast cancer, therefore, is about rallying that fear and that anger, using it for ballast in the sophisticated tug of war for donations. (Belkin 1996, para 9)

EMERGENCE OF THE AWARENESS CULTURE

The celebrity gala as well as the emergence of AIDS red ribbons as a fashion statement showed how the promise of preventative health communications advocated by scholars such as Backer, Rogers, and Sopory (1992) was overtaken by observances and awareness campaigns often symbolized by ribbons. As mentioned, we believe the need for funding, cause-related marketing, and the Internet formed the perfect storm to create the *awareness cul-*

ture. Quite frankly, the symbol of the *awareness culture* is, arguably, not so much ribbons as dollar signs.

At the same time researchers and health communication experts were learning how to design effective campaigns, corporations and marketers noticed the growing interest in health-related causes—such as the crowds at AIDS awareness events or the young people involved in Red Ribbon Week campaigns as part of the War on Drugs.

In *Pink Ribbons, Inc.*, Samantha King (2006) detailed how corporate influence and cause marketing brought breast cancer awareness to the forefront of America's health communication consciousness. Looking to tap into Americans' desire to "do good," many corporations searching for a campaign to support found their "dream cause" with breast cancer. Prominent companies included Avon, Estee Lauder, and AstraZeneca. In fact, AstraZeneca, the pharmaceutical company, was actually the force behind establishing Breast Cancer Awareness Month in 1985.

King (2006) argued that the fundamental purpose and approach to breast cancer remains similar to the 1930s' Women Field Army's "focus on early detection and treatment and reliance on traditional gender relations" (xiii). King questioned the efficacy of the approach, noting that a "woman's lifetime risk of breast cancer has increased from 1 in 22 in the 1940s to 1 in 7 in 2004" (2006, xviii). (In 2016, the National Breast Cancer Foundation said the risk was 1 in 8.) While many factors could play into this increased rate including better screening, King emphasized that rather than prevention, the research focus has remained on screening and treatment. She noted that the entities "at the heart of the cancer establishment have much to lose in terms of money and prestige if the tide were to turn away from the search for better therapies" (2006, xix). Among those with much to lose would be the Komen Foundation and AstraZeneca. King pointed out simply, "AstraZeneca is the manufacturer of tamoxifen, the best-selling cancer drug, and until corporate reorganization in 2000 was under the auspices of Imperial Chemical, a leading producer of the carcinogenic herbicide acetochlor" (2006, xxi):

> The success of AstraZeneca's campaign . . . is such that hundreds of organizations that are not official sponsors of NBCAM now also run breast cancer awareness promotions during October, almost always with the dual aim of promoting mammography and raising money. As such, NBCAM has taken on a life of its own and developed into a high-profile campaign for early detection ("awareness") and breast cancer charity produced by a disjointed but vast assemblage of players. (King 2006, xxi)

Harkening back to the successes of preventative health campaigns noted by Backer, Rogers, and Sopory (1992), we aim to encourage organizations that rather than try to emulate the "success" of NBCAM to instead bypass the *awareness culture* and develop campaigns that go to the heart of their cause—for prevention, eradication, or support, for example. We realize that foregoing name recognition and color-coded ribbons and wristbands goes against the prevailing wind, but our analysis demonstrates that (1) the breast cancer model is not actually as effective as perceived once the surface is scratched and (2) even for organizations that would like that sort of exposure, breast cancer remains entrenched as the favorite cause marketing of corporate America and will not be overturned anytime soon. At a minimum, we add our voices to those who are saying that ribbons are not enough and that awareness is overrated. Like Sulik (2012) in *Pink Ribbon Blues: How Breast Cancer Culture Undermines Women's Health*, we don't want people to feel "guilty for doubting a cause that was accepted as *overwhelmingly good*" (xxix). To this end, in Unit 2 we identify a number of myths associated with the *awareness culture*.

Going further, we call for a new model that bypasses the emphasis on awareness. Instead, we propose an approach that embraces participation, knowledge seeking/education, and recognition/involvement, while considering the aspects of communication that lead to commitment. We would like to see "raise awareness" edited out of the mission of health campaigns and replaced with what the organization is truly trying to accomplish, such as curing or treating a disease or providing social support. We realize this is a steep climb that could receive much pushback because of how ingrained awareness is into the educational and health communication campaign culture. And, the foremost reason the *awareness culture* is so pervasive is directly attributed to the pink ribbons of the breast cancer awareness and the pink ribbon culture that Sulik (2012) described. *Awareness culture* cannot be addressed until pink ribbon culture is understood.

Any discussion of how breast cancer came to the forefront of causes must include Nancy Brinker, who established the Komen Foundation in 1982 after her sister died of breast cancer, and who also points to the role of inadequate federal funding in the development of the *awareness culture*. The success of the Komen Foundation was not automatic, as Brinker recalled being dismissed by an executive of an underwear company when she tried to convince her to include mammogram reminder tags in bras. "It's negative advertising, and I'm in the business to make money," Brinker relayed the executive's statement to the *New York Times* (Green 1992, para 11).

The competition for federal funding was highlighted by Belkin (1996) in describing why the Komen Foundation had partnered with corporations to raise money and awareness. The 1996 article pointed to the success of Komen and other breast cancer organizations as building on other causes and being at the height of popularity "Like many a talented pupil, breast cancer learned from AIDS and then did its teacher one better. In the last few years it has become what AIDS could not—the darling of corporate America, which does not simply want to donate to the cause, but wants to embrace it completely" (Belkin 1996, para 45). Given the wave of ribbons from yellow for soldiers to red for AIDS and then pink for breast cancer, it's perhaps understandable that the breast cancer campaign sponsors enjoyed their time in the spotlight. "'This is our moment, and we have to make it work for us,' Brinker, the founder of Komen said. 'It didn't happen overnight, and it didn't happen by itself'" (Belkin, 1996, para 6). On the other hand, other causes were looking on, trying to learn from the success of the breast cancer campaigns. The *New York Times Magazine* article noted "vocal heirs apparent." The article that began with a gala in Dallas ended at a cocktail party on Fifth Avenue sponsored by *Harper's Bazaar*. The editor in chief of *Harper's Bazaar*, Liz Tilberius, who was battling ovarian cancer, watched as representatives of breast cancer organizations received donations. "'I'm fighting for the same recognition,' she said of that disease. 'Its time will come. We've not exposed it enough. We've not marketed the problem yet. These things take a little while'" (Belkin 1996, para 87).

Twenty years later, ovarian cancer is among the causes that have a ribbon—teal—but have not reached the exposure—dare we say awareness—of breast cancer. While it's understandable that other causes would like to learn from and overtake breast cancer the way breast cancer overtook AIDS, our premise is that rather than trying to emulate National Breast Cancer Awareness Month, health-related causes should bypass awareness campaigns in favor of more meaningful and tangible goals. No doubt, what King (2006) called "the consumption-based culture of organized giving" (xxvi) has become entrenched in health campaigns. "Satin ribbons and silicone wristbands of every color imaginable are worn to mark awareness of a myriad of issues ranging from breast cancer to 'troop support.' And Americans walk, run, swim, bike, and climb hundreds of thousands of miles each year to raise money for any number of charitable causes" (King 2006, xxvi). For example, it was somewhat surreal when Elizabeth, who tried to avoid discarded pink ribbons less than a year earlier, shared a teal tumbler from a sandwich shop that featured a ribbon in honor of National Ovarian Cancer Awareness Month.

In the face of growing competition for funding—both federal and from corporations and individuals—the proliferation of ribbons associated with health-related causes is a plausible outgrowth of the *awareness culture*. The organizations devoted to helping those affected by disease are trying to navigate the system that has developed.

Where Backer, Rogers, and Sopory (1992) called on health communication campaigns to use mass media effectively to build up like a "stalactite," the Internet has enabled constant communication, which enables year round "campaigns." The Internet has also enabled twenty-four hour-a-day fundraising on websites—and purchasing items for a show of support, namely ribbons.

Ribbons can be viewed as the symbol of the *awareness culture*, and now ribbons have taken on a life of their own and even become something of a cottage industry on the Internet. For example, Choose Hope offered twenty-seven ribbons for sale solely for cancer-related causes. Disabledworld.com said,

> Awareness ribbons are short pieces of colored ribbon folded into a loop, or representations of such, which are used in the United States, Canada, Australia, UK and other parts of the world as a way for wearers of the ribbon(s) to make a statement of support for a cause or issue. Due to their ubiquitous nature, ribbons have come to symbolize various concerns depending on the colors or the patterns used. Ribbons are now considered as a universal symbol for social or disease awareness, and a formidable path to a cure. (2016, para 3)

The site listed more than eighty ribbons but stated, "With new awareness campaign days, weeks, and months—as well as new ribbon colors, [sic] constantly being created, we are not sure how many awareness ribbon colors there currently are—but there certainly seems to be a lot!" (Disabledworld.com 2016, para 6)

The Ice-Bucket Challenge: Encapsulating the Awareness Culture in the Internet Age

The most prolific online awareness campaign is symbolized, however, not by a ribbon, but by a bucket. The Ice Bucket Challenge took the Internet by storm in the summer of 2014 and shattered previous fundraising efforts in support of ALS, or Lou Gehrig's disease. According to the ALS Association (ALSA) website, the challenge was created by a group of friends as a way to raise some money and create awareness while cheering up a friend with ALS. The idea was to challenge someone to make a large donation to ALSA or to post a video of a bucket of ice water being dumped on his or her head and submit a smaller donation to ALSA. Chris Kennedy, a professional golfer who made the initial challenge on behalf of an extended family member, said, "What started out as a small gesture to put a smile on Anthony's face and bring some awareness to this terrible disease has turned into a national phenomenon, and it is something we never could have dreamed of" (Sifferlin 2014, para 9).

The challenge went viral in the truest sense of the word, reaching all the way to the president of the United States, who declined to participate. Along the way, 17 million people are estimated to have participated by posting videos of buckets of ice water being dumped on themselves. One of the founders of the 2014 Ice Bucket Challenge, Pat Quinn, accepted a Webby Award in May 2015 for its viral success (Muscarella 2015). Acceptance speeches were limited to five words, and his statement "Every August Until a

Cure" became the impetus for a second-round Ice Bucket Challenge a few months later, though the 2015 version paled in comparison to the original, raising roughly $500,000 in the same time period that $78 million was raised in 2014 (Nodrum 2015).

By the numbers, there's no disputing the impact of the Ice Bucket Challenge. Visitors to alsa.org increased more than 7,000 percent, according to Similar Web in 2014. "Ice Bucket Challenge" made the Top Ten list of many news search sites. The campaign brought in a total of $115 million, in contrast to the $23.5 million ALS raised in 2013. Skeptics criticized the pace of use of the money, but Charity Navigator commended ALSA for transparency and thoughtfulness in taking a long view to address a problem that would not have an overnight solution given the debilitating and fatal nature of ALS (Wolff-Mann 2015). Another criticism was that only 10 percent of those who took the Ice Bucket Challenge in 2014 actually donated to ALSA (Maguire 2014).

At the time it was written, this section on ALS had to be revisited after waking up to news that the Ice Bucket Challenge was "trending"—a top topic on Twitter. Almost two years after the original Ice Bucket Challenge, in late July 2016, the ALSA reported that scientists had discovered another new gene associated with ALS that could lead to the development of new treatment. It was the third such discovery funded by Ice Bucket Challenge donations.

The gene discoveries are undeniably great news to be fully celebrated with hope toward improving treatments or even preventing ALS. A CNN story also used the 2016 discovery as an avenue to revisit the controversies surrounding the 2014 viral phenomenon. "Despite being heavily criticized for water waste and dismissed as a form of 'slacktivism' (lazy activism), many saw the Ice Bucket Challenge as a campaign driven by a passionate community that capitalized on peer-to-peer fundraising and activism" (Fawzy 2016, para 11).

Far from dismissing the Ice Bucket Challenge, we believe it is important and instructional on several levels. For one, the money raised was much needed due to the relatively small amount of federal funding, and the donations have been reportedly well used. As Wolff-Mann of *Time* wrote in 2015, when the second iteration of the challenge fell far short of the original viral sensation, "Even if most donors don't know what the letters 'ALS' stand for or anything about the illness, it's hard to look a $115 million gift horse in the mouth" (Wolff-Mann 2015, para 14).

However, we also believe the success of the challenge has been misunderstood and misapplied. Most importantly, the Ice Bucket Challenge was truly organic—it started as a challenge among family and friends, not as a corporate or organizational construct. In fact, *Time* reported that the challenge had been shared online before ALS was attached to it (Sifferlin 2014). ALSA is to be commended for capitalizing on the moment, and attempts to resurrect the challenge in second and third years are understandable, and perhaps even advisable—particularly after one of the challenge originators declared "Every August Until a Cure" when receiving an award. Writing in the *New Yorker* almost two years after the 2014 sensation but before the third gene discovery, James Surowiecki (2016) commented on the long-term benefits of the challenge and argued that it had achieved success from new donors and not at the expense of other charities:

> That, really, was the true accomplishment of the challenge: it took tools—the selfie, the hashtag, the like button—that have typically been used for private amusement or corporate profit and turned them to the public good. The campaign's critics implied that, had people not been dumping freezing water over their heads, they would have been working to end malaria instead. But it's far more likely that they would have been watching cat videos or, now, playing Pokémon Go. *The problem isn't that the Ice Bucket Challenge was a charity fad. It's that it was a charity fad that no one has figured out how to duplicate* (Surowiecki 2016, para 7, emphasis added).

We can agree that the challenge was—and perhaps remains—an incredible use of online tools. We can agree without a doubt that the money raised has been used for remarkable good. We can even agree, perhaps especially agree, that the challenge capitalized on tools that had been used for private amusement. And that's part of the issue to us. The challenge was based on amusement per the *awareness culture*. What we can't agree with is that the problem is that no one has figured out how to duplicate the "charity fad." For one, as stated, the Ice Bucket Challenge was a true organic, viral sensation that by definition cannot be orchestrated. Even a charitable fundraiser acknowledged that organizations had been contacting his company wanting their own "Ice Bucket Challenge," but it was simply not that easy. Jeff Shuck, the CEO of Plenty, told *Forbes*, "[I]t's not about the ice bucket. . . . You could sit in a room for a year and come up with a thousand ideas that seem like a breakthrough success, and then most of them wouldn't work" (Diamond 2014, para 7).

Most importantly and at the heart of our position is the sentiment expressed at the height of the original Ice Bucket Challenge by Julia Belluz writing in *Vox*. "Viral memes shouldn't dictate our charitable giving" headlined the story (Belluz 2014). "The ALS Ice Bucket Challenge, and its virality, raise some interesting questions about which charities and health causes we choose to give to. It seems to add further evidence to the fact that celebrities and gimmicks often drive our charitable donating more than, perhaps, they should," she wrote (Belluz 2014, para 5). A chart in the story contrasted the amount of money donated to causes compared to deaths by disease in the United States. Breast cancer topped the list of money raised while being fourth in deaths, for example. Prostate cancer was second in money raised while sixth in deaths.

Obviously, we support people giving to the cause of their choice. What we can't support, like Belluz, is giving that is dictated by viral memes and celebrities. Sure, it's tempting, much like Surowiecki, to consider that donations driven by fads are better than nothing, and that with slacktivism at least there is some good as opposed to playing video games. But, our concern is that with every viral meme and charity fad the *awareness culture* becomes even deeper rooted in amusement. Quite simply, far from being "better than nothing," we argue that giving based on viral memes contributes to a culture whereby rather than seeking out meaningful causes people wait until they are amused or entertained enough to join in—that they don't give until they are also in the spotlight themselves. We fully understand that in charitable giving, people are more likely to donate to causes that resonate with them. Our concern is that rather than seeking causes that are relevant, people might wait until a viral meme catches their attention or amusement, similar to what Postman described in *Amusing Ourselves to Death* (2006). Additionally, we don't believe charities should have to be in the business of brainstorming viral memes as a way to raise money to fund research on debilitating and fatal diseases. Even though the Ice Bucket Challenge did not use a ribbon, it definitely contributed to the *awareness culture*. Yes, we hear those like Surowiecki (2016) who argue that the Ice Bucket Challenge represents the reality of culture and social media today. We simply disagree that health campaigns should be dominated by amusement and viral fads.

A Call for Reclaiming Campaigns

We are calling for a new model of health-related campaigns and causes that bypasses the emphasis on awareness—and the accompanying amusement that we have found present through our research in the campaigns that will be presented in upcoming chapters. While observances may have their place, the *awareness culture* must be addressed. We believe communication scholars and practitioners are in a unique position to understand and effect change. Specifically, we would advocate that communication scholars and practitioners revisit the role of social science to be reminded that awareness was never intended as an end goal. As such, we would like to see awareness goals replaced with more meaningful, albeit perhaps difficult, goals. To that end, we have included in chapter 10 examples for improving writing mission statements and edited existing awareness mission statements as exemplars. In instances where certain behaviors have been linked to an increased likelihood of a disease, we call for an emphasis on promoting healthy lifestyles and nutrition as much as screening. We also encourage campaign planners to stop chasing "likes" and slacktivism and instead target publics that will become involved. Finally, we would like to see health campaigns and causes provide information that can empower those who are active and to disseminate information to others in their circle. Ultimately, what we are advocating is in some ways a reconsideration of Backer, Rogers, and Sopory's (1992) recommendation that campaigns build on social science theories such as Diffusion of Innovations (Rogers 2003) to effect adoption. However, our proposed model builds on and updates the Diffusion of Innovations model to take into account social media and its role in adoption—including factors which interact and lead to commitment. Behavior change is difficult, but it is what matters. And it's our goal.

Chapter Three

Awareness as Events, Observations, and Amusement

An Analysis of Selected Health-Related Websites

In an effort to gain deeper insights into the impact of the *awareness culture*, we conducted an analysis of selected websites to explore what features and tone were evident in health-related campaigns and causes. The campaigns/causes to be analyzed were chosen based on prominence, review of literature, and personal experiences. We had previously published studies on breast cancer and childhood cancer, which made them natural inclusions in the process. Prostate cancer was selected as a parallel to breast cancer. ALS was selected at the recommendation of the book publisher based on the prominence of the viral Ice Bucket Challenge in 2014. Finally, autism was selected because, like breast cancer, it has directly affected one of the authors and represents a cause that is ongoing. The purpose of the analysis was to look for common characteristics as well as to identify best practices in the websites of health-related cause organizations.

Selecting the individual websites for each cause was admittedly problematic in some instances. The criteria included the website that most closely represented the cause as well as relevance through an Internet search engine inquiry. In each case, the cause, such as "breast cancer awareness," was typed into a Google search engine. The resulting "hits" were noted, including those that were advertising supported. For breast cancer, the National Breast Cancer Foundation (NBCF) site, www.nationalbreastcancer.org, was selected. For prostate cancer, the Prostate Cancer Foundation (PCF) site at www.pcf.org was selected. For childhood cancer, the American Childhood Cancer Organization (ACCO) at www.acco.org was selected. For ALS, the

ALS Association (ASLA) at www.alsa.org was selected. For autism, the Autism Speaks site at www.autismspeaks.org was selected. In the case of breast cancer, childhood cancer, and perhaps autism, an argument could be made for selection of a different site such as Komen, St. Jude, or the Autism Society, but our criteria led us to the sites selected for the purposes of our study. Methodology of the data collection and analysis is included at www.theawarenessmyth.com.

NATIONAL BREAST CANCER FOUNDATION

NBCF Summary Description

We chose the National Breast Cancer Foundation (NBCF) site because of its specific association with National Breast Cancer Awareness Month (NBCAM) in October as listed on the NBCF website. The focal point of the site at www.nationalbreastcancer.org was a section of rotating photographs that encompass roughly a third of the visible site when displayed at 100 percent. At the uppermost left of the site, three tabs said "Awareness Month," "Donate," and "Fundraise." The color scheme was pink and white, with the logo including leaves. Donate was in pink; the other words were in white. A Facebook button (73k likes) and search bar were also in the top section. The second section included the anchor links "about Breast Cancer," "about NBCF," "our Programs," and "how You Can Help" (capitalization from site).

There were five distinct sections of the site, with the most prominent section featuring rotating photographs. With rare exceptions, smiling faces and stories of hope dominated the page. The next section indicated the mission, or at least purpose, of NBCF with the statement, "We provide help and inspire hope to those affected by breast cancer through early detection, education, and support services." Icons highlighted information about mammograms, education, support, and donations. The third section included an infographic that said, "1 in 8 women will be diagnosed with breast cancer in their lifetime," with a button to click to learn more about breast cancer. The fourth section offered three ways for people to help, including providing a mammogram, starting a fundraiser, and becoming a sponsor. The final section, which perhaps might be better divided into two sections even though visible on the same screen, included ways to stay informed such as signing up for a newsletter or to show support by shopping. Also visible were corporate sponsor logos, the site map, and approval seals from charity evaluator organizations.

NBCF Analysis and Discussion

The NBCF site was high on hope and help. "Hope" was found seven times on the first page. "Help" and "helping" were found ten times. The site also used "action" verbs on buttons, giving the feeling of doing something when a visitor clicks "start now" or "help now." The images and imagery were bright and upbeat, save for a "Tough Enough" photo featuring the Harley-Davidson logo. The people in the photos were all smiling—except for the serious "Tough Enough" biker shot in the same Harley Davidson photograph. Surviving was also clearly a theme—with even a caption about metastatic cancer referencing the patients as "inspiring."

Beyond hope and help and upbeat imagery, ribbons and the leaf logo of NBCF were also prominently featured. The leafy iconography arguably communicated life and perhaps even growth, while the ribbon was associated with breast cancer awareness. Various shades of pink on a clean white background highlighted the symbolic color of breast cancer month. The language used on the buttons and headlines was consistently in active voice with action verbs such as "start," "join," and "help." The first buttons following the scrolling pictures seemed to sum up the overall purpose of the site—"learn now" and "donate." The social currency on the site seemed to be information and actual money. There were statistics and multiple opportunities to sign up to receive newsletters or hear about programs. Additionally, whether by actually donating or organizing a fundraiser or even shopping, one of the main actions visitors were called to do was contribute in some way.

In comparing the NBCF site to lessons from previous research and specifically Diffusion of Innovations, there appeared to be an indication of inviting decisions by the prevalence of buttons that encourage the reader to "engage in activities that lead to a choice to adopt or reject the innovation" (Rogers 2003, 164). For example, the site invited visitors to click to "learn," "donate," "shop," "give," and "read more," among others. However, at the first page level, which the description showed contains ample elements, the site did not move on to implementation or confirmation. It's even debatable if the site provided "how-to knowledge." Through clicking, visitors could in fact "do" something, but there was little description to consider what the action will mean or how it could lead to an eventual outcome.

Considering social learning, the message was that of happy survivors and cheerful helpers. Again, there was one photo that could be described as "tough" in fitting with the Harley Davidson brand, but most photos showed smiling faces. Those looking to the site for examples of how to proceed in the face of breast cancer would learn to model behavior that promotes smiling, giving, and shopping. On the main site, before clicking through, there were no examples of how to live or cope beyond hope and being an inspiration.

The stated mission of NBCF was "to help women now by providing help and inspiring hope to those affected by breast cancer through early detection, education and support services." Breaking those elements down, the imagery could definitely be seen as hopeful and perhaps inspiring. It's feasible that clicking through would result in help, but what sort of help is not evident on the window to the world that is the front page of the website. Early detection was mentioned through an early detection/calendar link and a button for mammograms, but no additional information was given. There was not even a brief description of why or what do to or how to get a mammogram. There was a link to specifically provide a mammogram to a "woman in need." There were certainly elements of education presented such as "learn more" and "read now," but what the visitor would be learning is not described. There was an application available to download called "Beyond the Shock," which provides "educational resources with informational videos, stories from breast cancer survivors, and a community Q&A." While this seems helpful, why must visitors have a smartphone or mobile device to go beyond shock? If there was another way to access the information, it was not readily available. And, again, perhaps understandably, the focus is on survivors, but not everyone survives.

Similarly, while there was a support button, the support being offered was not clarified. Was the support for women with breast cancer? Was it for family members, friends, or caregivers? It might be all, but it was not obvious. A person "affected" by breast cancer, as the mission says, would have to go on a scavenger hunt of links trying to find helpful information. Beyond the infographic "1 in 8 women will get breast cancer," there was little information. For example, there was no talk about nutrition or causes or risk factors. "Research" and "treatment" links were only seen in the site map, indicating they were in the drop-down menus. There was a pep rally feel, and that might well be the intended tone. In fact, the tone might even be successful for the given purposes in keeping with the evident *awareness culture.*

The site also fed into *awareness culture*, specifically the Pink Ribbon Culture Sulik (2012) described. Because the mission was to support early detection, perhaps the tone was appropriate in that there is a prevailing belief that there is almost always cause for hope with cases of early detection. What about those who aren't hopeful or happy? Does the NBCF provide support for them? Rather than truly diffusing information or providing social learning for how to navigate a breast cancer diagnosis, the site brought to mind Postman's (2006) *Amusing Ourselves to Death.*

The point of this analysis was not to be critical of the NBCF's mission or its execution. The goal of the analysis was to highlight how the ribbon/awareness culture permeates campaigns—or perhaps more accurately observances. The NBCF site was well designed and attractive and likely a positive influence to its given target audience. We would hold, however, that the site does not truly move beyond awareness as so many hold in defense of awareness campaigns.

PROSTATE CANCER FOUNDATION

PCF Summary Description

The Prostate Cancer Foundation (PCF) website was found at www.pcf.org and had a primarily white background with blue and orange accents. The site was considerably shorter than that of NBCF, with all content being displayed in three screens. At the time of the analysis, the dominant image was of hundreds of people in dress clothes gathered between columns and flanked by PCF banners. The caption said, "Count Us in Mr. Vice President—#WECANSERVE. PCF Salutes Cancer Moonshot." The reference was apparently to President Barack Obama's 2016 State of the Union address in which he mentioned the Cancer Moonshot initiative led by Vice President Joe Biden to increase cures for cancer, but no direct explanation was provided. The PCF logo is blue with an orange curved stick figure beside it and the motto "Accelerating the world's most promising research." Also visible on the opening screen were multiple buttons to donate, the PCF logo and blue ribbon, and multiple links.

The page was divided into two columns, one wide and one narrow, with the group photo being in the wider column. At the top of the right column beside the group photo was a blue box with two ribbons superimposed with Major League Baseball (MLB) logos flanking another emblem of two bats with a baseball and the words "HOME RUN CHALLENGE." The box was apparently referring to the MLB partnership with PCF, but no explanation was given. Underneath the baseball box was another lighter blue box that said, "QUESTIONS ABOUT CANCER? Find your answers here." Also viewable without scrolling down was a section with rotating photos and headlines. The first was a photo of Joe Torre, wearing an MLB cap and identifying him as a "Hall of Famer." The headline said, "Watch Our New Public Service Announcement Featuring Joe Torre." The other photos included a group shot of dozens of people, none clearly identifiable; a photo of colorful fruits and vegetables, with the headline "Healthy Habits for Living with Prostate Cancer: Download or Order Your Copy"; and two head shots of men, one in a lab coat and one in a suit. The headlines mentioned studies and treatments.

Scrolling down led to a "New and Noteworthy" section. For example, one headline read, "Prostate Cancer Foundation and Major League Baseball Step Up to the Plate to Raise Awareness and Fund Research for Prostate Cancer." Another announced, "Obesity and a high-fat diet promote prostate cancer progression by amplifying the activity of cancer genes." Four smaller boxes offered information for nutrition, fundraising, free guides, and partner-sponsored trials. The bottom of the site featured an "ask the doctor" link and a box that said, "Shaped by Experience. MOVember." A site map, social media links, and charity badges anchored the site.

PCF Analysis and Discussion

The Prostate Cancer Foundation website was mainly straightforward. There were many links to click to "learn more." There were several references to stories about research, diagnosis, and treatment. There were also multiple links to donate. Visually, the site was primarily modular with orange and blue text and emblems—particularly ribbons.

In terms of awareness, at first consideration, the PCF site seemed to provide ample information—to expose the visitor to enough knowledge to lead to a certain level of understanding in keeping with Diffusion of Innovations (Rogers 2003). In contrast to the breast cancer site reviewed, on the surface there was a serious or at least straightforward tone, including tips for living with prostate cancer as well as linking to symptoms. However, a closer analysis called into question if the information available reached Rogers's (2003) "how-to" level of awareness-knowledge. In other words, there was a lot of "what" but not quite so much "how." Additionally, there were top-of-the-page featured references to MLB without an explanation of Major League Baseball or what benefits PCF or those affected by prostate cancer might receive. The picture of bats and balls and the reference to picking your team—with no reason why—called to mind amusement (Postman 2006) and even entertainment and definitely reinforced the *awareness culture*. While the partnership with MLB might well be advantageous to PCF, the positioning made it seem more like a game, even in a site with an overall serious tone. Similarly, the first featured photo is a former baseball player and manager. Using a celebrity might be a good way to draw interest, but it was unclear what the message was as the headline merely said to watch the public service announcement featuring Joe Torre. The site did provide links to a nutrition guidebook and a reference to supporting men's health, but again these were not clearly explained.

It was not immediately clear who the primary target audience of the PCF site was. Perhaps it was those with prostate cancer or their caregivers. Or, with the emphasis on newsletters, perhaps the site was designed to function as a resource bank for media or those seeking information about prostate cancer. Alternatively, the site could be a way to raise money through donations.

The motto of PCF is "accelerating the world's most promising research." How the website does that was not immediately clear. PCF is to be credited for going beyond fluff and hype by providing information about symptoms and living with cancer. The site even touched on politics by mentioning the vice president's Cancer Moonshot, although a reference for context would have been beneficial. The site was not all hope and hype—or fun and games. However, games were still part of the cause in the form of baseball, and the role of MLB could—and we advocate should—be more explicitly explained. While some might see a natural link between prostate cancer and baseball, not all men are baseball fans—and certainly not all caregivers or loved ones of those with prostate cancer would recognize a former professional baseball player and manager. If Joe Torre is going to get top billing over the researchers and nutrition, the site should at least give a frontline reason why and how his presence accelerates the research and mission.

AMERICAN CHILDHOOD CANCER ORGANIZATION

ACCO Summary Description

The American Childhood Cancer Organization (ACCO) page was found at www.acco.org. It opened to a screen dominated by a photograph of a child. In fact, there were five close-up, rotating photos of children, each that dissolved after four seconds. The photographs were not exactly candid but also not studio. The children were a mix of ages, gender, and ethnicity. Some seemed to be in a hospital room. One was wearing an oxygen tube.

Blue and gold were the primary colors on the page, including the logo, which brings to mind both a ribbon and an adult hugging a child. In the top center, in a children's type font, were the words "because kids can't fight cancer alone®." There were also contact information and social media sites as well as links to join, donate, contact, and a search bar.

The ACCO website was by far the lengthiest of the ones analyzed, and again the full description can be found on our website at www.theawarenessmyth.com. There are nine distinct sections, mainly informative and most likely geared toward family members or those affected by childhood cancer. There were numerous photographs and links about how to help, awareness, resources, donations, and a store.

The second section of the page welcomed visitors to the site and said, "Childhood cancer kills more children than any other disease in the United States today, yet treatments designed for a child's body remain frustratingly out-of-reach." A paragraph describing the ACCO followed, including that it was founded by "parents who themselves have faced this challenge." The site devoted a large section to a musical campaign designed to promote childhood cancer as an "international child health priority."

There were multiple mentions of partners, including how to receive a free hat for "your warrior." In the middle of the partner section was also a link to a 24/7 peer support line. The following sections emphasized resources and programs, including promoting gold ribbons and fundraisers to provide pajamas for children with cancer. A somewhat distinctive feature of the ACCO was that it allowed for local divisions to start personalized nonprofit foundations. The site continued with promotions for the "Go Gold Tee Shirt Campaign" as well as other fundraisers and ways to commemorate September as Childhood Cancer Awareness Month. Other programs mentioned were "Gold Awareness," "Hero Beads," and "Gold Ribbon Hero." Each section included photographs, often featuring children or young people modeling the product or program.

The next sections were more informative, including a graph showing the "Time Spent by Family Caring for Child with Cancer." There was also a Latest News and Live Newsfeed section, including a reference to the "Moonshot to Cure Cancer" and "Help us remind Vice President Biden that children face cancer too!" while referencing President Barack Obama's State of the Union address that mentioned committing to finding a cure for cancer. The latest news scroll had dozens of headlines, ranging from fundraising events to research studies to features on a parade and links to "more campaigns." The page was anchored with invitations to join a mailing list, take a survey, and find a local group, along with quick links, a blog, site map, and contact as well as a badge from the Better Business Bureau Accredited Charity and social media links.

ACCO Analysis and Discussion

There was a certain dissonance on the ACCO page, which was likely inherent and understandable in that it is a page about childhood cancer. The phrase "'child' and 'cancer' should not be in the same sentence" kept coming to mind during the site analysis. The slogan "because kids can't fight cancer alone!®" was featured in a comic sans, cartoon-type font. The phrase has trademark protection. The rest of the site had primarily a more serious tone. Pictures of children were not all smiles, although there were certainly grins. Still, the smiles were on the faces of kids who had lost their hair and were often wearing tubes or ports. This is not to say that the site was dismal, but it was also no pep rally. Even the gold seemed dim. There was perhaps some defiance—or maybe resilience, starting with a photo of the toddler with raised clenched fists to open the page. But there was also a nod to normalcy—kids being kids, with mentions of pajamas and popsicles.

Notwithstanding the comic font at the top of the page, the content was serious. "Read more" and "learn more" buttons highlighted the informative content, maybe even to the point of being overwhelming. Then again, the page said the ACCO was founded by parents, so if the target audience was parents, then it was understandable that there would be an abundance of information. On the other hand, if the target audience was comprised of parents and immediate families, then there also was a dissonance in the multiple donation buttons. It seemed a bit incongruent to be asking for monetary donations inches away from "learn more" buttons about treatments or peer support. Additionally, if the site was geared toward families, it would seem that some of the programs—such as peer support—would receive greater priority in location on the website.

If the site was indeed primarily aimed at parents or families, then the site was addressing a level of awareness-knowledge Rogers (2003) mentioned but not so much "how-to knowledge." It's possible that deeper in the site such information was available, but that was not clear. More clarity could help families widen the support circle and move from aware to active publics in Grunig's terms. For example, the pajama campaign looked to be something meaningful that could be an "action" a group could take to support children with cancer, but it was largely lost and had to compete with many other elements. Moving the information up and streamlining it could help families share it with their support communities. Similarly, it was not clear why the peer helpline was so far down the page and why it was part of the "partners" section.

Even in a mainly serious and informative website, the ribbon and *awareness culture* were evident again. The ACCO page, in fact, specifically mentioned the gold ribbon as "unfortunately" not being well known yet providing an opportunity to raise awareness about childhood cancer. This is not to say that the amusement phenomenon has infiltrated causes supporting childhood cancer. They are kids, after all, and it makes perfect sense that parks and picnics would be featured. Still, the "donate" and even "shop" buttons again added a bit of dissonance.

The site layout was modular, largely text driven with candid photographs. It was not exceptionally polished or filled with iconography, which added an air of authenticity. ACCO was described as "uniquely committed to improving the lives of children and families living with cancer and its long-term side effects, as well as bringing ever-greater awareness to the need for new, more effective treatments appropriate for cancer's youngest warriors." The site highlighted programs and provided information to that end. Information about research and treatments was less evident than that about programs, however. There also was information given—such as the effects of childhood cancer on the employment status of family members—that was powerful but did not have a clear call for others to help—or how to help. There was a definite emphasis on advocacy in saying the Cancer Moonshot initiative should not forget childhood cancer. Similarly, the Child4Child campaign is designed to use the voice of children singing to "remind policymakers, scientists, industry, and indeed the world that the time has finally come to make childhood cancer an international child health priority!!" How the campaign would be disseminated was not clear on the front page, though there was a link to learn more. It appeared the purpose of the mention on the site was to recruit children to be part of the song campaign.

The ACCO mentioned multiple times that it wanted to raise "awareness." It also called it unfortunate that the gold ribbon is not better recognized. The ACCO seemed to be wanting more attention from researchers and government funding to address childhood cancer—which is understandable. What we see as unfortunate is that the *awareness culture* is so pervasive that the childhood cancer cause would need to go with the route of ribbons and awareness to gather support.

Perhaps the main issue with the site was a disconnect between design and strategy, or perhaps designers and coders did not fully recognize multiple target audiences. To be fair, the researchers would not want to be the ones building the site. Former students of one of the researchers are parents of a child who was diagnosed with cancer—and a researcher had recently read a blog that their baby girl couldn't be in the sun because of chemotherapy treatments before her first birthday. The researchers hope the ACCO or similar sites provided help and support, yet also wonder if it could help more. Would there be a way she could link "ways to help" in her blog? Although our methodology only called for what was visible on the front page, we hovered over the "We Can Help" link at the top of the page. It included sections "For Kids," "For Teens," "For Families." These links could be highlighted and prioritized, rather than part of a bar with ten other links. Then again, those needing the resources might cut through the clutter to find them.

ALSA

ALSA Summary Description

The ALS Association (ALSA) website was found at www.alsa.org. When coding began in late spring and early summer 2016, the site opened to a dominant photograph of a pen sitting on top of an Emergency Preparation Checklist form. Underneath the photo in white letters on top of a blue background, the caption said, "Are You Prepared? Three steps families living with ALS can take to prepare in case of natural disaster." However, before coding was completed in mid-July, the photo changed to a picture of a red bucket with the ALS logo on it, filled with ice piled high and overflowing. A superimposed caption to the right said, "Every drop adds up" while white text in the blue background this time said, "Make the impossible happen . . . again. This August and every August until there's a cure." There were buttons "Help Find a Cure DONATE" and "Learn More." Additional links visible on the landing page were "About ALS," "About Us," "Our Research," "In Your Community," "Advocate," "Get Involved," and "Donate."

The ALSA page was in the middle of the sites analyzed in terms of length, with eight distinct sections, primarily in a white background with red and navy text or iconography. Social media links and the red "Help Find a Cure DONATE" stayed anchored on the left side of the page. The mission—"Leading the fight to treat and cure ALS through global research and nationwide advocacy while also empowering people with Lou Gehrig's Disease and their families to live fuller lives by providing them with compassionate care and support"—was in the second section. Boxes below the mission included links for "Latest Research," "Find Services," "Take Action," and "Raise Awareness." The boxes included icons overlaid on top of photographs.

The next sections invited readers to "Join the Movement to End ALS" by joining a "Walk to Defeat ALS®," which included a group photo of people in red shirts with their hands in the air. The second way to join was to "Advocate" and included a button that said, "I Will Advocate." Finally, there was a link to learn more about the National ALS registry, with a picture of a man in a baseball uniform the researchers recognized as Lou Gehrig.

A section on "Patient-focused Guidance for ALS Drug Development" came before the "Resources" section. The resources section said, "Whether you're newly diagnosed, navigating your journey with the disease, caring for a person with ALS, or researching the cure, there are resources to support you," and provided links to reading material, conferences, and grants, for example. The site included an "In the News" section with two stories and a link to more news. The next two sections were to connect with the organization and to "Give Now" to "Help Create a World without ALS."

The bottom of the site included links for a site map, press room, FAQ, privacy policy, link policy, RSS feed, and to contact us as well as a statement of permission from Lou Gehrig with a registration mark and a link to www.lougehrig.com. There were also badges from nonprofit organizations.

ALSA Analysis and Discussion

The ALSA site can be described as clean and consistent—even professional. The splashes of red on a white background brought to mind a medical and even healthful tone, arguably augmented by the iconography that used medical and scientific symbols such as hearts and microscopes. The site was geared for information, with multiple "Learn More" buttons. It was also geared for giving, with a "donate" button anchored as the page scrolls as well as additional "donate" and "give now" buttons. The site also featured advocacy, acknowledging the important role of government funding and the importance of keeping the need in front of Congress.

ALS has been best-known as "Lou Gehrig's disease" so it's somewhat interesting that he was not featured until near the bottom of the page. However, there was a notice at the very bottom of the site that permission was granted to use his likeness, so it was understandable that ALS wishes to build recognition separate from the late baseball star.

When coding first began on this site, the most striking fact was that the "Ice Bucket Challenge" was not referenced on the site. Even with the change in the photograph displayed, the term "Ice Bucket Challenge" was still not mentioned, although the dominant image was of a bucket with ice chunks piled high above the sides. The researchers did a web search and found the challenge embedded in the ALSA site, but there were no direct links—from "get involved" or "donate" buttons found. The picture of the bucket was unmistakable, however, as was the tag "Every August Until There's a Cure." The Ice Bucket Challenge fundraising phenomenon will be discussed in subsequent chapters, but it's interesting to note here how prominent the photograph was as well as how little attention was given to the challenge on the page. The picture itself was questionable given that a bucket that full of ice would be difficult for some to lift and that much ice could be dangerous to dump on someone's head. In fact, it's somewhat surprising that there was not a disclaimer or caution—or even a photo with people modeling a safe way to do the challenge.

There were clearly marked resources for different groups—for people with ALS and caregivers, researchers, and healthcare professionals. It's notable that resources for people with ALS and their caregivers were together. Also notable, and we would say commendable, was that the resources mentioned were for caregivers rather than specifically family, which can seem exclusive. The different resources were clearly marked, but they were in the bottom half of the first page. More prominent placement could be beneficial.

The website was not driven by those with ALS or even really talk of their stories, so there was not much in the way of social learning or modeling. "Raising awareness" was mentioned twice. The most common theme likely was of finding or fighting for a "cure," which was eight times. There were three mentions of some form of "treatment," which could speak to help in living with ALS, as well as two each for "fight" and "end." As far as calls to action, there were buttons for such actions as "learn," "attend," and "advocate."

An analysis of this site with the emergency preparedness feature photo would have a different tone than that with a landing page devoted to a bucket with ice in it. In most all other ways, the site was informative and provided resources. The only other nod to entertainment or amusement was participation in a walk, but even that description focused on honoring those with ALS. The photograph of the ice bucket did not. We find it unfortunate that an otherwise well-organized site came to be dominated by a photo of an ice bucket and what it represents. We understand that a photo of a disaster plan is not as eye catching, and we definitely understand the need for funding for research and that the success of the original Ice Bucket Challenge in terms of dollars donated is not debatable.

What is debatable is the sustainability and appropriateness of using what some see as a social media stunt and slacktivisim to raise money and "awareness" when there is some evidence that many of those taking part in the challenge didn't know what cause was being supported. We addressed some aspects of the Ice Bucket Challenge previously, and a full discussion of the Ice Bucket Challenge is outside of the scope of this analysis, but it's also essential to understanding how health campaigns have moved from being educational and providing "how-to" knowledge to providing amusement and entertainment. Again, the point of this discussion is not so much to criticize ALSA for going back to the well, or bucket as it were, for money, but to ask how health causes got to such a state and what could/should be done about it. "Awareness" was only mentioned twice on the ALSA site, and there were no ribbons symbolizing awareness—yet there is likely no more clear example of the *awareness culture* than the Ice Bucket Challenge. What does it say about our culture that such a debilitating disease as ALS caught "lightning in a bottle one year" as a social media fad but then fundraising and participation plummeted the next?

AUTISM SPEAKS

Autism Speaks Summary Description

Autism Speaks was found at www.austismspeaks.org and was represented by a blue puzzle piece at the left top of the page. The landing page background was white with "Walk," "Donate," and "Shop" blue links centered in blue letters across the top complete with accompanying icons of a person walking, a heart, and a shopping cart. The top of the page also featured a section called "Vitals" with links to "Autism App," "Resource Guide," "What Is Autism," "Screen Your Child," and "Tool Kits." The dominant image was of the United States in green, with the blue puzzle emblem in the corner. The caption said, "State insurance mandates increase access to affordable autism care." The copy underneath added, "Autism Speaks issues statement in response to positive findings and need to overcome remaining barriers to care." Drop-down menus at the top of the image were for "FAMILIES AND ADULTS," "RESEARCH," "ADVOCATE," and "GET INVOLVED." There was also information based on age and safety information to "Make This Summer Safer with Safety and Wandering Prevention Resources" as well as other "help resources" and links for questions.

The Autism Speaks site was among the shortest of those analyzed, divided into four vertical sections. The puzzle piece and buttons above the map image stayed anchored at the top of the page. The remaining page was divided into four columns, all with blue text on a light gray background on top of the white page. The columns were "SCIENCE NEWS," "ATN@work:Autism Treatment Network," "Why I Walk," and "Science@Work." There was an image anchoring each column. Three of the images included children and had superimposed copy such as "Learn the Signs," "Wondering What to Do," and "Early Access to Care." The fourth image was a light blue, cloudlike background with the autism puzzle piece, three light blue autism bracelets, and a blue autism shirt. Blue text in the top left corner says, "Get Your Autism Speaks Gear Today!" and there was a blue "shop now" button at the middle bottom.

"GET INVOLVED" headlined the next section. Ways to get involved included finding a walk, attending an event, supporting corporate sponsors, and advocating in your state. Again, each column included a photo, ranging from a bouncy house, to serving food, to corporate logos, and a capitol building. A dominant image in the section, one that took up the width of the page rather than being in a four-column spread, was of several women walking, holding a banner that said, "For Jake's Sake" with the autism puzzle pieces flanking it. The image included a link to find a walk.

The bottom of the site had information about the "Autism Response Team (ART) members (who) are specially trained to connect families with information, resources and opportunities. They are available to answer calls and emails from 9am to 1pm local time." The section also included links to "More About Us," "Around the World Links," and to connect through social media. Three badges from charity organizations were at the bottom of the page.

Autism Speaks Analysis and Discussion

The blue puzzle piece was among the most common elements on the Autism Speaks site, showing up at least eight times. What wasn't evident was a mission of Autism Speaks or why the puzzle was chosen as its emblem. The site seemed to be designed with those who are already part of the autism community in mind, as it had information about insurance and safety guides. There were multiple photos, but they were small and hard to see in detail. The site was largely driven by articles, with informative and news headlines requiring a click to read more. It was not immediately clear from the headlines to what extent the articles would provide "how-to" knowledge, but there was definitely an emphasis on science and relaying research information.

There was also an emphasis on walking—the autism walks to be exact. In fact, the word "walk" was featured on the site the same number of times as the blue puzzle piece, making it a prominent feature. Scrolling through the site, there was never a time that the word "walk" could not be seen on the researcher's screen. There was information on "why" people walk as well as "how" to find a walk. Additional prominent features were shopping for gear as well as donating. Somewhat striking was that the emblem beside the donate button was a blue heart. Again, the site seemed to be targeting those that are already somewhat engaged with autism on some level. The possible exception could be the links to "screen your child" and "learn the signs," but even those tabs pointed to family or those who would be involved in care rather than those on the edge or outside of the community.

The autism ribbon and awareness month were not highly visible on the site, although there was a link for World Autism Awareness Day. The impact of the ribbon and *awareness culture*, however, can arguably be seen in that "Walk" and "Shop" were highlighted top and center on the page. "Walk" was the single biggest feature, and "shop" could be considered the second most frequent call to action. The Autism Speaks site was straightforward and informative. But, it wasn't immune to the *awareness culture* of being event driven and showing pictures of smiling people walking at rallies. While the symbol was of a puzzle, the missing piece might very well be helping caregivers of those with autism be equipped to explain to others about their circumstances and what help they most need.

SUMMARY OF SITES:
COMMON CHARACTERISTICS AND BEST PRACTICES

There was something of an irony in that each website mentioned awareness at least once given that readers would have already been aware on some level to find—or even look for—the site. The Internet, however, is one of the factors we've identified as contributing to creating the *awareness culture* in which observations have overtaken campaigns. As opposed to mass media, which Rogers (2003) identified in Diffusion of Innovations as being effective at the awareness level, websites are static and appear from our research to serve as a "one-stop shop" to meet multiple target audiences with different needs and interests. The case study analysis reinforced our belief that health-related causes are adversely affected by the *awareness culture*.

In terms of common characteristics, the analysis showed the websites are steeped in the *awareness culture* through an emphasis on shopping, sponsors, observances and events, rather than prevention. Granted, not all causes lend themselves exactly to prevention; that is, a discussion of nutrition as a way to prevent childhood cancer or autism does not seem appropriate. However, it does for breast cancer. And while the PCF did mention nutrition, it was not exactly prioritized. Instead, the sites at times presented "life and death" issues in a "fun and games" light. While we understand the need for fundraisers and that the events can be forms of social support, we also find that the approach contributes to the idea of causes as amusement. We saw no explicit campaign goals. While research and resources were mentioned, there were no clear steps to move from what Grunig and Hunt (1984) would call aware publics to active publics—short of clicking to learn more or donate, for example. While perhaps implied, a sustained commitment to the health-related causes was also not always explicit—with the exception of the PCF and ACCO. Both PCF and ACCO referenced the Cancer Moonshot, an initiative to find cures for cancer.

Again the nature of websites and trying to serve multiple target audiences presents a difficult situation, and we did identify some best practices we would recommend. We applaud references to nutrition, prevention, lifestyle and healthy living tips, and community support. We also find that the websites provide a suitable repository for news and information.

In summary, we recognize that the sites were trying to meet multiple needs and the accompanying pressure to create a certain tone to encourage donations and participation in the current *awareness culture* environment. However, we think the move from goal-oriented campaigns to observances as reflected in the sites was a move in the wrong direction from the identified successes in health communication campaigns. Raising awareness has reached mythical proportions, but we argue that health campaigns based on awareness are steeped in myths. In most cases, awareness has already reached a benchmark, or visible level, and instead campaigns should focus on "how-to knowledge" or steps toward implementing beneficial or preventative action. In the next section, we further identify specific myths of awareness campaigns.

Unit 2

Chapter Four

The Awareness as Education Myth

As stated in chapter 1, according to the U.S. Department of Health and Human Services, there are more than two hundred national observances for awareness days, weeks, months, and so on. In addition to months, most causes have their own "awareness" agenda, often tying awareness and education together implicitly or explicitly. For example, a statement for United Nations Entity for Gender Equality and the Empowerment of Women (2012) reads, "Public awareness and education are essential to changing social and cultural norms which perpetuate harmful practices." Likewise according to the Prevent Cancer Foundation, "The Prevent Cancer Foundation Awareness Campaigns are designed to help educate the public about specific preventable cancers." Additionally, the National Heart, Lung, and Blood Institute has a web page specifically called "Education and Awareness" with a description of several health programs. Although the web page states that the organization uses scientific knowledge to inform publics so that people may make choices leading to positive health outcomes, awareness is often used as a goal.

The supposition that an awareness campaign educates its intended audience on a particular situation or condition is often incorrect or incomplete. For example, a search for the term "autismawareness" on Facebook yielded seven unique pages with a combined total of 3,237,950 likes. Using the hashtag #autismawareness on Instagram yielded 771,502 posts while the hashtag #autismawarenesstoday yielded 46,954 posts and #autismawareness month yielded 75,902 posts and the list goes on. Autism awareness, like many health awareness campaigns, is prevalent at this point. But, what do we really know about autism spectrum disorder (ASD) despite the awareness efforts? How has autism awareness helped educate us about autism?

Despite autism awareness efforts, many myths and misconceptions exist about ASD. The School of Education at Johns Hopkins University lists several of them. For example, it is a myth that autism is a behavioral/emotional/mental disorder. ASD is actually a developmental and neurobiological disorder that manifests in childhood. Another myth is that people with ASD have "savant" skills but in reality most people with ASD do not. Yet another myth is that people with ASD do not want to socially interact but in reality they may want to interact but do not know how. The list goes on.

Myths and misconceptions abound for a variety of conditions. For example, the National Breast Cancer Organization identifies several myths about breast cancer such as that having the BRCA1 or BRCA2 gene means a person will definitely get breast cancer when in reality not everyone who carries the gene will get breast cancer and breast cancer may be caused by reasons other than those genes. Furthermore, in regard to prostate cancer, it is a myth that prostate surgery causes urine leakage. The recovery time may take a while, but within a year 95 percent of men will have full bladder control. In addition, though the *Washington Post* listed five myths about ALS (Rothstein 2014), despite the well-known Ice Bucket Challenge (e.g., ALS is caused by sports; ALS is a disease of old people), people would be hard pressed to know what the acronym ALS (amyotrophic lateral sclerosis) stands for (Wolff-Mann 2015) and many people may not know enough about the disease to have misconceptions about it. According to a *Time* article (Davidson 2014), high-profile participants in the Ice Bucket Challenge (e.g., Matt Lauer on the Today Show) did not even mention the disease.

All too often, awareness campaigns simply call attention to the fact that certain situations/conditions exist, but stop there and do not result in educating or informing publics. One could argue that the ALS Ice Bucket Challenge did not even result in the most basic awareness. As stated by Davidson (2014) in a *Time* article, "In an age where hashtag activism and information-free awareness are becoming more and more common, we should be very conscious of how people make viral trends as useful as possible."

This is due in part to two reasons: (1) the meaning of the term "awareness," and (2) confusion of tools with content in a society where entertainment is packaged as information and education.

THE MEANING OF THE TERM "AWARENESS"

Let us examine the meaning of the term "awareness." According to Merriam-Webster Dictionary online (2016a), the word "aware" is defined as: (1) knowing that a situation/condition/problem exists; (2) feeling, experiencing, or noticing something; or (3) knowing and understanding. Synonyms of "aware" include "cognizant," "conscious," "sensible," "alive," and "awake."

Other than being cognizant/conscious of a condition or situation, the definition seems to rest on knowledge. "Knowledge," according to Merriam-Webster (2016b), is defined as: (1) information, understanding, or skill that you get from experience or education; or (2) awareness of something, the state of being aware of something. Synonyms of "knowledge" are "learning," "erudition," and "scholarship." Although the word "knowledge" may refer to being cognizant of something, it seems to rest on an *understanding* of a condition/situation. A definition of "understanding" refers to a mental grasp or power of comprehending subjects, according to Merriam-Webster (2016c). So, it would appear there the term "awareness" might imply either cognizance or knowledge. These nuances may fuel confusion in how to use the term "awareness" so that a health organization can conduct a successful awareness campaign focused on simply alerting their target audience of the existence of a condition or situation without actually informing or educating them beyond that. So, any campaign aimed at increasing awareness can be successful by its very existence. People can wear a certain color or participate in walks and wear ribbons and never go beyond the aim of making people cognizant of a condition/situation. One can argue that such cognizance can be the first step to education but that assumes a multiphase campaign leading to real education.

An examination of advertising models depicts awareness as a first step in the persuasion of consumers. For example, in the AIDA model (Hackley 2005; Mackay 2005) awareness leads to interest, which leads to desire, which leads to action. In the DAGMAR model, awareness leads to comprehension, which leads to conviction, which leads to action (Mackay 2005). It would appear that in this model the term "awareness" does mean cognizance. The model seems to suggest that in order to persuade, it is necessary to gain the attention of the consumer, and once this is achieved, the consumer can be informed/educated, which leads to conviction and then action. Thus, "awareness" can be used interchangeably with "attention" in this model (Mackay 2005). The same is true of the Lavidge and Steiner (1961) model, which begins with awareness. In this model, awareness leads to knowledge and proceeds to liking, which leads to preference and then conviction and then finally to purchase. The models are all hierarchical models and are very similar to one another. A main difference in the Lavidge and Steiner's model from AIDA or DAGMAR is that it is more specific and elaborate, but all models assume that one step leads to the others. However, Lavidge and Steiner acknowledge that persuasion may occur over time, certain steps may be passed, and that consumers may purchase in any step of the model. For example, a consumer may intend to purchase one product but if the product becomes unavailable, the consumer may purchase a different product.

The model that offers the most sophisticated conceptualization of awareness and its relationship to knowledge is Rogers's *Diffusion of Innovations*

(1962, 2003). An innovation is defined as "an idea, practice, or project that is perceived as new by an individual or other unit of adoption" (12). Rogers began with education as a starting point for the adoption of ideas, practices, or projects. The theory posits that the decision-making process occurs in five stages: (1) Knowledge: Person becomes acquainted with and acquires knowledge of an innovation; (2) Persuasion: Person develops positive or negative attitudes towards an idea or product and seeks more information; (3) Decision: Person moves toward adoption or rejection of an innovation; (4) Implementation: Person uses an innovation; (5) Confirmation: Person evaluates the innovation and continues to use or rejects the innovation. This process is affected by several variables (e.g., characteristics of one's social system such as social norms, personality variables of the receiver such as attitude toward change and perceived need for the innovation) and results in differences in whether or not people adopt the innovation and how fast they do so.

It is important to further consider how Rogers conceptualized knowledge in his model. He specifically discussed three types of knowledge (2003, 21): (1) awareness-knowledge: occurs when a person realizes an innovation exists and can lead to motivation for gaining how-to knowledge and principles-knowledge; (2) how-to knowledge: consists of an individual learning how to use an innovation properly—more complex innovations require greater how-to knowledge; (3) principles-knowledge: consists of the principles and theories of how the innovation works—if an individual adopts an innovation without adequate principles-knowledge, the likelihood of misuse or discontinuation of an innovation becomes more likely. Thus, in Rogers's model, awareness is one part of knowledge and it is knowledge that will lead to eventual adoption of an innovation. Rogers then discusses adopter categories in terms of how quickly individuals will adopt innovations: innovators, early adopters, early majority, late majority, and laggards (2003).

It is important to note that awareness is not an end in and of itself in any model and attempts to make awareness as a goal are misguided. In regard to health campaigns, when little is known about a health situation or condition, awareness may provide some needed exposure, but after a campaign has gained attention, it would seem the focus should be on education, which should guide calls to action. Awareness can only go so far. For example, Jacobsen and Jacobsen (2011) stated that a primary goal of the National Breast Cancer Awareness Month (NBCAM) was to encourage breast exams so that the disease could be detected early. In their research, they found that NBCAM was initially effective in increasing November diagnosis rates, but that there is "little evidence that the NBCAM led directly to increased diagnosis in later years" (60). The authors speculated that women are now more likely to get routine screenings, and as such, the authors stated that some of the decline in screenings may be due to "awareness saturation" (61). Jensen et al. (2014) also found that three-fourths of the individuals in their survey reported "cancer information overload," which made it difficult for respondents to know what information to act upon.

Jacobsen and Jacobsen (2011) recommended that well-established health campaigns focus more on the benefits of increasing fundraising or enabling support groups rather than simply focus on early diagnosis. They further recommended that research should identify what types of awareness campaigns are most successful in achieving outcomes for different segments of the population. While there may be benefit in all those approaches, as Pezzullo (2003) stated in an article called "Resisting National Breast Cancer Awareness Month," the NBCAM campaign has focused on screening and support but has done little to shed light on causes of cancer.

Many popular health campaigns could benefit from exposing people and making people cognizant of a situation or condition, but once this has been achieved, education can ensue. An examination of Diffusion of Innovations sheds light on the role of knowledge in decision making and how it affects behavior.

CONFUSION OF TOOLS WITH CONTENT

Epistemology is the study of the nature of knowledge. The term "epistemology" comes from the Greek word *episteme*, which means *knowledge*, and *ology*, which means *the study of*, so epistemology literally means the study of knowledge. Epistemology goes beyond what we know to asking how we know what we know. Neil Postman (1985), in his book *Amusing Ourselves to Death*, stated that a medium such as human speech, the written word, or television affects the content of messages. He argued that "writing freezes speech" (12) so that as people are reading they may stop and ponder certain points, they may reread, look for errors in the writing, and think abstractly about what they are reading. As such, the written word encourages logic and reason and produces discourse that is coherent, serious, and rational. Television, Postman's focus in the book, on the other hand, produces a conversation in images where "the overarching presumption is that it is there for our amusement and pleasure" (87) and is a "theatre for the masses" (28) leading people to be "sillier by the minute" (24). Although Postman was concerned with television in particular, it seems reasonable that the same logic can apply to the tools and techniques of health awareness campaigns which result in a pseudo-understanding of a health problem but not in true education.

This is primarily because the tools and techniques that campaigns employ become the campaign in and of itself. When we think of awareness campaigns we may think of a cause or condition like breast cancer, but we immediately think of the techniques involved in the production of the awareness campaign like brochures, walks, events, press releases, mailings, etc.

For example, the phrase "think pink" focuses on the tools of the campaign and not education about breast cancer.

In an article titled "Communicating about Cancer Through Facebook: A Qualitative Analysis of a Breast Cancer Awareness Page" Abramson, Keefe, and Chou (2015) examined how a popular Facebook cancer awareness campaign functions. By analyzing the Facebook posts on the page, the authors found that posters used the page for a variety of reasons such as expressing personal opinions, telling personal stories, promoting and advertising products and services, giving and seeking information and support, and encouraging other posters to participate in breast cancer screenings. The authors noted, however, that even when encouraging participation in breast screening endeavors, there is little breast cancer health information education provided on the page they analyzed. In fact, some posters even provided incorrect health information that went unchecked such as one post indicating that becoming vegetarian and working out would prevent cancer, which may have some merit but should be qualified. The authors noted that a main feature of the Facebook page was the encouragement of online shopping in order to promote breast cancer research. The authors made a conclusion that "awareness raising is not through provision of health information or consumer education, but rather persuasive techniques to encourage donation and camaraderie" (240). This raises the question of the purpose of a health campaign in general.

In the persuasive models discussed, the end result is the purchase of a product. In a health awareness campaign, the end result is not the purchase or donation per se but should lead to a goal of eradicating a disease and healing sick people or providing services or relief to those suffering with or affected by a health condition. This is why a *New York Times* article titled "A Growing Disenchantment with October Pinkification" cited Karuna Jagger, the executive director of Breast Cancer Action, as saying, "A lot of us are done with awareness. We want action."

But a great deal has been invested in awareness, which will not lead to real education because the nature of awareness campaigns encourages feeling and emotion. Health awareness campaigns have their own epistemology that results in only the most basic understanding. And while some argue that the most basic awareness may in fact lead to pursuit of actual education, this does not occur due to people thinking they have actually become educated or been supportive by being aware. They can click "like" on Facebook or attend one event and be "aware," which is known as "slacktivism" (see Hill and Hayes, 2014). The notion of awareness as engendering emotion and feeling can be seen in an article in the *NonProfit Times* (2013) called "10 Elements of an Awareness Campaign." The elements are as follows: "Ignites from a strong emotion; Establishes personal value/purpose for the organizers; Ties process to the outcome; Grabs attention at the launch; Captures imagination along the way; Focuses on passion more than leader(s); Designs it to spread; Makes followers matter; Ends with a big goal; and, Creates a measurable difference." All ten are parts of an awareness campaign, but other than ending with a big goal (which is often unclear), education is not part of the campaign.

A Google search of the words "awareness campaigns" provided examples of many awareness campaigns. *Top Design Magazine* provides examples of thirty of them. We will use three as examples of how these ads gain attention but provide little education, despite being considered "awareness" messages.

(1) A Salvation Army advertisement: The copy reads, "Poverty Shouldn't Be a Life Sentence" and features a mother sitting in a chair and holding her school-age child close in what appears to be a basement with marking on the wall keeping track of the days gone by. Underneath the Salvation Army logo, the copy reads, "Giving Hope Today." The ad provides a website address and phone number. The message in the ad is presumably saying that people do not always need to live in poverty.

However, how is poverty defined? Does a person have to live in dank, dark conditions in order to be in poverty? And what services would the Salvation Army provide to help people out of poverty? Is the purpose of the ad to get people to donate to the thrift stores? Is the ad encouraging people in poverty to call the Salvation Army, and if they do, what will they be told? Will they be given applications for social services, money, the address to a food bank, free clothes, help with housing, and so on?

(2) The Aware Helpline: The ad features a man with an arm coming out of his mouth gripping the face of a woman who is turned away with an anguished expression. The small copy at the bottom reads, "Verbal abuse can be just as horrific but you don't have to suffer in silence. Call the Aware Helpline for Advice and Support, dates/times/number."

What is the awareness in this advertisement? It would seem that the main message of that ad was that person being verbally abused can be helped and does not need to suffer and that the number provided could help. However, what type of help is available? What can people who are being abused expect when they make contact? Who is on the end of the telephone line? Furthermore, what constitutes verbal abuse? In the image, it's being equated with violence. People may be in an abusive relationship, but if it isn't violent, they may not know it.

(3) Adam Le Adam: An elderly woman sits in a chair knitting a noose. The copy reads, "Over 50% of all suicides are committed by senior citizens." There was text that appeared to be in a language other than English in the bottom right corner. So, we Googled the copy and found the ad along with an organization called "Adam Le Adam." However, we were confused when we tried to search for "Adam Le Adam" on Google, because rather than discovering an organization focusing on suicide, we found a website looking for

young adults to volunteer to improve relationships within the Jewish-Israeli community.

Aside from the sponsorship of the ad, we wonder what the organization wanted to accomplish with this simple point. Did they want more support services for elderly people with depression? What type of support services? Did they want people to look for suicidal tendencies in the elderly? And how would those tendencies be identified since most elderly women do not knit nooses, so people would need to know signs of depression and suicide in the elderly?

These are only print advertisements and may be a part of larger campaigns. However, an analysis of these advertisements, which were classified as awareness campaigns, leaves us with impressions and feelings but certainly not with education. Yet, people may feel self-satisfied that they took steps to be aware.

By calling something an "awareness" campaign, it is likely it will result in ribbons and walks and likes, but, in the end, those are superficial. An epistemology of an "education" or "information" campaign may have different results. There is a point in the learning process that a person must move through stages of learning and encounter complexity but awareness campaigns are not set up for complex or thoughtful thinking. Postman (1985) said that television gave us a world where information must be entertaining and that television, which is visual, is not conducive to logical, orderly, and coherent thought. It is the same with awareness campaigns. If the way we know about problems and conditions is through awareness, we are constantly "amusing ourselves to death," as Postman said regarding television. We need to ask ourselves what means will best convey the information we need to be communicated. We need to ask ourselves what constitutes knowledge in a world of awareness. Are we, as a society, okay with cursory knowledge being considered education because the packaging is fun and entertaining and makes us feel good with minimal effort? At the very least, society needs to ask these questions.

Chapter Five

The Awareness Is Enough Myth

"We've got to get the word out." "If people only knew." "We need to make people aware...."

Awareness campaigns can be traced to the Women's Field Army, or "khaki brigade," that went door-to-door informing women about breast cancer in the 1930s. By the twenty-first century, awareness had reached mythical status. "Creating awareness" dominated mission statements of health-related organizations and cause-marketing programs of corporations. Create enough awareness, it seemed, and problems would be solved—or at least addressed along the way, surely. The ubiquitous nature of breast cancer awareness months, observances, and fundraisers can make it hard to argue against the success of the awareness campaigns at face value. And, who could blame other causes for wanting to duplicate the success of the pink ribbon campaigns? But, rather than agreeing with the mythical status of awareness, we came to see awareness as a myth.

For a time, we soft-pedaled our uneasiness with awareness, saying we weren't against awareness, that it was a needed starting point—it just wasn't enough. The problem with acknowledging the importance of awareness, however, is that far too many times awareness has been the end goal. Granted, there is no shortage of 5K races or other fundraisers that raise money for a cause. Yet all too often the goal, as seen in mission statements in the websites we analyzed as well as observances listed on the U.S. Department of Health and Human Services website, is simply to "raise awareness" about a disease or condition. Occasionally there has been a call for screening or a preventative measure in the mission statements, but more often than not there has not been a call to action or any action or behavior to change. The wording of the mission statements is an example of how, as discussed previously, health-related causes have developed an *awareness culture* in which preventative or behavioral change campaigns have given way to observances. Exposure has been substituted for true awareness knowledge, so that the goal was to be seen, with no further development.

The author of *Pink Ribbon Blues: How Breast Cancer Culture Undermines Women's Health* was quoted in the *New York Times* as saying that individual purposes must be considered for each cause and campaign:

> "You have to look at the agenda for each program involved," (Gayle) Sulik said. "If the goal is eradication of breast cancer, how close are we to that? Not very close at all. If the agenda is awareness, what is it making us aware of? That breast cancer exists? That it's important? 'Awareness' has become narrowed until it just means 'visibility.' And that's where the movement has failed. That's where it's lost its momentum to move further." (Orenstein 2013, para 40)

The unease we felt about awareness campaigns crystallized with the reading of Erin Santos's (2013) article, "Awareness . . . What a Bullsh*t Word." Santos, whose seven-year-old daughter had died of cancer, took issue with campaigns such as Childhood Cancer Awareness Month. While others clicked "like" on a Facebook post or considered signing up for a race, she lived daily with the loss of her daughter. How did awareness help that? Comments to her article showed that, rather than help, it actually hurt. People who had been affected by childhood cancer personally found awareness campaigns lacking in action and even contained a level of misinformation.

Santos didn't say awareness was a good start. Santos didn't say that she was glad more people knew about childhood cancer. She said awareness was a problem. She went so far as to say that while it was good that the "C" word could now be spoken thanks somewhat to previous awareness campaigns, "awareness" now is an obstacle to progress.

"Cancer is an epidemic in this country and I'm confused as to why people aren't freaking out more than they are. Probably because they don't have it . . . yet. Or maybe because we are all so 'aware' of cancer, but aren't taking action against it" (Santos 2013, para 11).

The rapid increase and even success of awareness campaigns has created the myth that awareness is enough—which is at the heart of the *awareness culture*. Awareness as enough encapsulates several facets, and this chapter focuses on two main myths: (1) that awareness automatically inspires some action, and (2) that being aware equals a form of enlightenment and ultimately leads to improvement. Discussion of the myths will mainly center on individuals and their roles. Yet, those individual responses are undoubtedly in response to the *awareness culture*, which has been built and sustained by health-related campaigns and corporate-cause marketing. As with so much related to the *awareness culture*, the Internet and celebrities also play a role.

As far as awareness automatically inspiring action, few say that they firmly believe that awareness is truly the end goal. They tend to say that, of course, there should be action, but that awareness has to come first. Educators—including our colleagues and reviewers of previous publications—pointed to models such as AIDA—Awareness, Interest, Desire, Action—and Grunig and Hunt's (1984) publics to emphasize the importance of awareness, with "aware" being the step between "latent" and "active." As noted in Unit 1 and discussed in the Education Myth, we included the AIDA and Grunig and Hunt (1984) models as well as *Diffusion of Innovations* (Rogers 2003) in considering the role of awareness, or knowledge-awareness in the case of Diffusion, in our literature review for case studies related to awareness.

The models have a linear focus, and while we are not fans of such lock-step approaches, we also recognize their value in providing a potential explanation for cognitive and behavioral actions. But taking the linear models at face value highlights the Awareness Is Enough Myth. In these models, awareness is a gateway, a pass-through, on the way to end goals such as taking action or changing beliefs. Even in these models, energy and effort are focused on leading people *through* the model to reach an end-point. Once attention is gained, there is an effort to spark interest, promote desire, and prompt action. Moving outside of health campaigns, in selling merchandise like shoes, a company might purchase television advertisements to create awareness, hoping for interest that will lead to a desire for the product and ultimately an action in the form of the purchase of a product. Even granting that the purchase decisions can follow such a linear pattern, the same arguably isn't true for health campaigns. What exactly is the interest or desire related to diabetes, for example?

Similarly, Grunig and Hunt (1984) described publics as latent, aware, or active. Latent publics aren't aware there is an issue or problem. Aware publics have knowledge of an issue but are not participating. Active publics are engaged and taking action in a meaningful way. For example, in a local referendum, a latent public might not be aware of a ballot initiative to raise sales tax to improve roads. An aware public might have heard of the initiative but not formed an opinion. An active public would at a minimum vote for the initiative but also take part by asking others to support it. Putting this model into a health campaign—as seen in the website case studies—it is hard to imagine that there is a very big percentage of people in the latent public group when it comes to most forms of cancer, particularly breast cancer. However, rather than putting resources into moving the critical mass of people in the aware public group to the active public group, campaigns continually focus on awareness, which becomes self-perpetuating awareness without developing action. We understand that there are those who sincerely believe that if people are aware of a need, then they will act on it. It's not clear to us, though, if the goal of the unending and annual awareness observances is to make the small number of people who aren't aware to become aware—think in terms of Rogers's (2003) adoption curve in the Diffusion of Innovation—or if the goal is to make the people who are aware *more* aware in hopes that additional information will eventually inspire action. It might well be a moot point. As Sulik (2012) intimated, in the *awareness culture*, awareness has given way to visibility—and really not much more.

Regardless of the intention, awareness is not enough, and Santos (2013) is not alone in saying that action is needed rather than awareness. In a 2014 *New York Magazine* article headlined "Awareness Is Overrated," Singal said that we were living in a "golden age of awareness-raising" (2), adding that attempts to raise awareness were more visible and more a part of everyday life than ever. But the article questioned the premise of the awareness campaigns. "The underlying assumption of so many attempts to influence people's behavior—that they make bad choices because they lack the information to empower them to do otherwise—is, except in a few cases, false. And what's worse, awareness-raising done in the wrong way can actually backfire, encouraging the negative activities in question" (3). The article quoted Victor Stretcher, a professor at the University of Michigan's School of Public Health, as saying, "We've known for over 50 years that providing information alone to people does not change their behavior" (4).

Despite the fact that many awareness campaigns have already hit a critical mass and studies have shown for a half century that knowledge does not lead to action, awareness campaigns thrive and grow. While various aspects of the National Breast Cancer Awareness Month have been criticized, other campaigns continually seek to reach that level of ubiquity. The question is: Why? Perhaps they are trying to capture lightning in a bottle, or perhaps bucket, as in the ALS Ice Bucket Challenge, which started as a grassroots effort among friends and sprung up to raise more than $100 million in the summer of 2014 in a truly viral phenomenon (Wolff-Mann 2015).

In her blog "The Story of Telling," Bernadette Jiwa (2016) described volunteers holding buckets and blocking entrances to a market while asking for donations in what she described as a "one-off" attempt at fundraising. She said, "[B]y inviting people to pay volunteers to go away, the charity loses" (2). She encouraged tactics that generated more involvement and commitment. She summarized, "It turns out that getting people to notice us is rarely the biggest problem we face" (4).

Evidence of ineffective health education awareness campaigns is, unfortunately, abundant. Singal (2014), in *New York Magazine*, said, "There are examples everywhere" (4). The article's list of ineffective campaigns began with an anti-drug campaign, which actually increased the likelihood young people would try marijuana. Our own field notes include a personal anecdote from a colleague who knew of teenagers who began doing drugs after being introduced to them through an anti-drug campaign. Other examples included in the article were diabetes campaigns, bullying, and even filling out federal financial assistance forms. Awareness campaigns simply weren't all that effective.

The evidence about the limitations or even repercussions of awareness campaigns begs the question of why awareness campaigns are instituted at all. The simple answer is that sometimes they are, or at least were, necessary and important to reach a baseline level of what Rogers (2003) might term "awareness-knowledge." The example *New York Magazine* gave was in connecting smoking to lung cancer. A more recent example could be the Zika virus. But, beyond initial information, why do awareness campaigns continue and proliferate?

Our study leads us to believe that people engage in awareness campaigns, or more precisely observances, because they have to do *something*. Whether it's personal or a community event, awareness campaigns can give a feeling of empowerment, of making a difference, of taking action even in the face of limited results. We also found that the awareness campaigns sometimes offered a form of social support, such as for the seminary student who moved from the middle of the country to the East Coast after her mother was diagnosed with early onset dementia and found comfort in a monthly Alzheimer's support group, despite not being in full support of the mission of #endAlz. They do so because in the *awareness culture*, there has developed a sort of social norm for participating in such events—even if those most directly affected might not always see the benefit. At times, the "doing something" mind-set, however well intentioned, can actually have adverse affects. We recognize that people affected by various health-related conditions are at different stages and have different levels of appreciation, and resentment, for awareness campaigns and observances. For example, a friend who knew we were writing this book sent us the Facebook status of her friend who has diabetes. She obtained permission for us to use this post:

> When I was a child, every coin I threw into a wishing well went in with the hope that someday I wouldn't have diabetes anymore. My mom would ask me what I wished for and I would tell her, "to not have diabetes." She would smile kind of sadly at me and I never understood why. Now I do. Wishing that my diabetes will go away is never going to work. Hoping, praying, pleading, bargaining and all those other stages of acceptance are never going to work. The reality is I am not the invincible 10 foot tall giant I think I am inside my own head. My body doesn't work right and I have to live with that every day. So excuse me if I don't care about that Race for the Cure event or those paper JDRF shoes you buy at the grocery store or any of those fundraising things people do because they want to "help." I'll be over here dealing with the reality of my situation and doing the best I can with what I've been given. If you want to help, [try] talking to a diabetic. Ask them how they're doing and what you can [do] to support them in their struggle. Don't just throw your money at some "good cause" because it's what you think you should do.

These powerful words seemed to hit squarely with our Awareness Myth premise. Then, the very next day, the same inbox had another message from the same friend. "The day after one FB friend has a rant about awareness, I have another one promoting one," she said. The public post was a memory describing a rare disorder associated with the Autism Spectrum:

> Today is the day we celebrate and raise awareness for all families that live with this disorder day in and day out. O is one of 200 people in the WORLD with this genetic disorder. Please read the stories and post that I will share today. We hope soon to start a foundation and begin raising money so more research can be done for our kiddos. It is the most frustrating thing in the world that doctors have never heard of this and don't know how to help your loved one. Our kids deserve better than this. Thanks to everyone who supports us, family, friends, therapists. Your love and support mean the world to us.

Obviously, there is a huge difference in a disease that affects two hundred people in the world and breast or prostate cancer that affects one in eight. There arguably is a baseline need for awareness-knowledge, particularly how-to knowledge, for those in the medical field especially to know about a rare disorder, but what of non-medical publics? How does awareness help a situation of a genetic disorder? As one respondent said, "We can't work on something as a society that we don't know exists, but knowledge of problems and problem solving skills are NOT the same thing." Contributing to the issue is the fact that raising awareness reaches its potential ceiling and plateaus quickly. "The problem, though, is that once a certain level of awareness has been raised, there are rapidly diminishing returns to raising more of it," Singal (2014, para 10) wrote in *New York Magazine*.

It's notable that the person posting about the rare condition associated with autism thanked people for love and support, which leads to another example from our observations of why awareness isn't enough.

Michelle, a personal friend of one of the researchers, had just turned forty when she noticed tightness and soreness under her arm. There was a little lump, but she thought it was a pulled muscle. She was still a few months from her baseline mammogram and thought she would wait. A decade previously, her mother, a heavy smoker, had been diagnosed with lung cancer. A few years later, her mom was diagnosed with breast cancer. Michelle's younger sister, a coach and physical education instructor, pleaded with her to go for a mammogram, and when she did, she learned she had an aggressive form of stage three breast cancer. She went to MD Anderson in Houston for treatment, including chemotherapy and a double mastectomy. Michelle wore pink ribbons and was touched when the college softball team coached by her sister wore pink ribbons to go with their green uniforms in her honor. So, the researcher was a little surprised when Michelle shared a Facebook post that was a photo of a breast scarred from cancer treatment.

"Here's your fucking breast cancer awareness," the post from pushinginthepin said. A follow-up comment said, "This was during my 35 day radiation treatment back in 2013. Breast cancer isn't sexy. It's not about saving boobies. It's not about no bra day, which is really just an excuse for women to post sexy pics of their nipples pressing through their clothes. It's scars, nausea, pain, bald heads, burnt skin, and broken hearts.

"If this doesn't make you 'aware' then I don't know what will.

"Does it make you uncomfortable? It should."

In an interview, a researcher asked Michelle what she had in mind when she decided to share the photo. She took a deep breath and said,

> "People needed to see it, you know? People needed to see it. There's more to it. It's hard. They need to think deeper than just posting things or saying they support something. It wasn't all that gruesome but it got the point across. There's so much more you never think about . . ."
> "Even when mom had cancer, I didn't think about it until it happened to me. I'm a strong person, but the chemo knocked me on my ass. Now when I hear someone has cancer, I wonder about their friends and family. If they have people to help them, cause you can't do it by yourself. You can't work. It takes so much effort to get to your treatment. People never think about all the money for travel and meals."

She shared the cost of an experimental drug. Her insurance paid 80 percent, but even that left her with almost $100 a pill. She received a voucher for another 80 percent off, leaving her with $400 a month for the treatment. She shook her head and said, "It just takes so much."

A friend had been listening quietly. "All this about awareness," her friend said. "How about a tank of gas?"

Awareness Myth #1 is Awareness Is Enough. And, part one of that myth is that awareness inspires action. As Michelle's story shows, even for those most directly affected, no level of "awareness" can be guaranteed to help others, or even themselves, know what to do—or to do it if they do.

The second part of the Awareness Is Enough Myth is that awareness equals enlightenment and therefore leads to an improvement in the situation. There is almost a self-centeredness in responses to awareness campaigns. There is no behavior to change. No call to action. Nothing to do or really be gained. Just be aware. Informed. Be a little more knowledgeable than the next person or at least than you were before. The working title of this section once was "Awareness Is a Parlor Game," but that struck a little too close to home, because sometimes academics are guilty of getting caught up in spouting numbers and making the trivial seem substantial—or vice versa. Such "one-up-manships" can be common in faculty meetings or gatherings, and apparently academics aren't alone.

"Think of the last time you were at a party and shocked your fellow guests with some dire statistic about the black-white incarceration divide or global warming or poverty in Brazil," Singal of *New York Magazine* challenged in "Awareness Is Overrated" (Singal 2014). "What you felt at that moment probably wasn't just empathy or sadness at the state of the world. No. If you're honest with yourself, it mostly felt good to be the bearer of bad tidings. You were helping to raise awareness" (1).

Calling the statistics dire first seemed like a stretch to even the researchers. Startling, maybe. But dire? Then our team looked closer and reviewed the data from our website analysis. The statistics were indeed presented in an alarming fashion; that is, "1 out of 8 women will be diagnosed with breast cancer in their lifetime" and "Childhood cancer kills more children than any other disease in the United States." We noticed that even awareness-knowledge (Rogers 2003) can have a sensational feel to it, as if shock value were needed to draw attention and gain visibility. And, perhaps shocking statements are needed to gain attention given the competition for exposure with more than two hundred observances listed on the U.S. Department of Health and Human Services site.

Beyond providing knowledge or information, awareness campaigns often involve a sort of sensationalism, intended to incite a gasp, to draw attention and spark conversation. Take, for example, the bulleted statistics and bold infographics that highlighted additional websites in addition to those in our analysis of websites.

The American Diabetes Association provided the following information on a fact page:

- "1 in 11 Americans has diabetes today.
- Every 23 seconds someone in the U.S. is diagnosed with diabetes.
- 86 million Americans are at risk for diabetes.
- Diabetes causes more deaths than AIDs and breast cancer combined" (This Is Diabetes 2016, 1).

The Alzheimer's Association site said, "Alzheimer's disease is the sixth-leading cause of death in the United States and the only cause of death among the top 10 in the United States that cannot be prevented, cured or even slowed."

The National Association for Continence said, "Over 25 million are affected by incontinence."

These are just a few examples, and the conditions and statistics are of varying levels of severity and presented with differing levels of urgency. The American Heart Association (AHA), somewhat ironically, put a rather positive tone on information that heart disease is the number one killer in the United States. "In fact, heart disease deaths have declined so steadily over the decades that we are eagerly awaiting the day when it is no longer the leading cause of death in the U.S. We've already seen the stroke death rate drop—from the No. 3 cause of death in the U.S. to No. 5 over just five years," AHA (2016, 2) said on its website at www.heart.org. Then again, perhaps it is understandable to credit the generosity of donors with research that has led to increased survival rates and prevention efforts. Other statistics truly are dire—and heart breaking—such as that from the American Childhood Cancer Organization (ACCO), which states on its Childhood Cancer Awareness Month page that "in the U.S., 15,780 children under the age of 21 are diagnosed with cancer every year; approximately 1/4 of them will not survive the disease" (2016, 1).

The ACCO site added, "A diagnosis turns the lives of the entire family upside down." The impact, the upside-down life, addresses the faces behind the numbers. Turning lives upside down brings to mind the statement of Erin Santos, whose daughter died of cancer: "Cancer is an epidemic in this country and I'm confused as to why people aren't freaking out more than they are. Probably because they don't have it . . . yet. Or maybe because we are all so aware of cancer, but aren't taking action against it" (Santos 2013, 11).

Through the two hundred–plus observances mentioned on the U.S. Department of Health and Human Services site there are near constant reminders and statistics of diseases or causes to be aware of. The flip side of Awareness Is Enough is much starker than parlor games. Because, for all the examples of Trivial Pursuit–type facts that awareness campaigns promote with breathless fervor, there are real people struggling with the diseases and issues the campaigns purport to support. Under the sensational statistics, someone is suffering. The one in eight means that someone is hurting, and those stories aren't always told—or at least they are often whitewashed or pinkwashed in the case of breast cancer. That's not to deny the need for positive, uplifting stories. It is to suggest that personal stories are sometimes lost in campaign glitz or fear tactics.

A social media post from a man whose mother died of brain cancer poignantly encapsulated the Awareness Is Enough Myth. His wife handed the printed Facebook post to a researcher during a conversation about awareness. His words struck at the core of the *awareness culture*. They also pointed out, similarly to Michelle's, that even those who think they are informed or aware do not, and perhaps cannot, fully feel the impact. That is no one's fault, necessarily. We, similar to him, are not taking issue with anyone's motivation. However, there are unintended and sometimes adverse consequences to awareness activities and observations, and we believe it is incumbent upon communication scholars and practitioners to acknowledge a broader audience that is not enamored with awareness and to make it a priority to stop reinforcing the *awareness culture*.

His post pointed to the impact the Internet and celebrities have on the *awareness culture*. Speaking about a country singer who was dying of cancer, he wrote that he would be glad the talk about the singer would "be over soon. I'm not downplaying their love, or cancer. But as millions weep for a person they don't know, I wonder how many know the struggle, having to help your sister basically care for a full grown infant, because you promised not to put her in a home." He continued, talking about taking his mother to chemotherapy treatments, making sure medicines don't get mixed up, sitting up at night, and treating bed sores. The awareness observances, frankly, rubbed him the wrong way. "Wear your damned ribbons, buy all the pink shirts and feel better about yourselves. Have you been there? Some have."

He recounted arguing with family members and lying to his mother because "the cancer in her brain has her delusional" and "sitting in the doc's office while he tells you there's nothing else they can do." And then, in something of a twist, rather than saying he hoped people would realize what they were saying, he said exactly the opposite. "For all those that THINK they know, that are sad cause she's [the celebrity singer] gone, that silently weep someone dying they didn't know or don't know first hand what cancer can do, I hope you stay ignorant. . . . For all those that know the struggle, pain, agony, and relief, God bless you."

"*I hope you stay ignorant. . . .*" For all the talk of awareness, here is a man who at age twenty-eight lost his mother to brain cancer and was hoping others would never know the same feeling. Like Michelle and Erin Santos, he knew that until you experience the disease first-hand, you can't truly empathize. Some say, "knowledge is power." Others believe that "ignorance is bliss." The truth could be both, in the middle, or neither. Our research leads us to conclude that "awareness" has taken the status of a "cure-all," a sort of "sociological placebo" as described in an interview. A social norm seems to hold that as long as people have been exposed and that the cause is visible enough, then that visibility will lead to action and enlightenment—which will somehow bring an improvement. In other words, the *awareness culture* of observations promotes the myth that Awareness Is Enough. We say it's not. Awareness isn't always even a good start. If it were, as Santos (2013) said, then as a society we would recognize the epidemic and address it beyond a month observation. To summarize the respondent whose mom was diagnosed with early onset Alzheimer's, if awareness were enough, then as a society we would do more than acknowledge the problem but actually prioritize solving the problem.

Chapter Six

The Awareness as Acceptance Myth

"I'm watching all these people at work and try to relate [to them] but how can I? I can't have a normal life. They are all so lucky. If I started to talk [about it], it wouldn't do any good. They could never understand the scope of it, how deep it goes. All aspects of life are colored with frustration and utter exhaustion" (Journal of Marceline Hayes, May 12, 2011).

Above is an excerpt from my own journal that I briefly undertook in order to help come to terms with raising a child with autism and all the frustrations it entails. I had begun trying to use writing as a form of self-therapy after reading an article by James Pennebaker (1997) on writing as a therapeutic process. I believe this quote demonstrates my feelings of isolation and feelings of misunderstanding and lack of acceptance of my situation parenting a child with an autism spectrum disorder (ASD). There are many such sentiments I expressed in my journal. I wrote once, *"Things other parents take for granted? Going to a restaurant with a 10 year old without there being food all over the floor"* (June 11, 2011).

There are also examples of interactions with others where I felt totally judged and diminished and invalidated. For example, *"Someone came to our house this morning to tell Steve [my husband] that my kids are running off into someone's yard while we 'sleep' and taking stuff. Steve told her Dylan had autism and she said 'He [my other son] doesn't and informed him that she knew all about it because she was a school teacher and knew all about autistic kids. I wish he would have told her, 'No you don't you only think you do. Come back when you actually know something.'"* (May 17, 2011). As a parent I have felt like an outsider with other parents and peers, and of course, my child struggles with acceptance in spite of autism "awareness." In some ways, I think the autism awareness movement has added stress to parenting my child with autism.

It is estimated that one in sixty-eight children has an autism spectrum disorder (ASD), according to the Centers for Disease Control and Prevention (CDC). ASD refers to a group of developmental disorders characterized by impairments in language, communication, and behavioral challenges, according to the National Institute of Mental Health (NIMH; 2016). ASD is a spectrum ranging from high-functioning cases to more severe cases where people are entirely non-verbal and unable to care for themselves. According to the CDC, some examples of signs and symptoms of ASD are avoiding or not making eye contact with others while talking, appearing to be unaware of others even when being addressed, repeating or echoing words and phrases over and over, repeating actions over and over, unusual sensory reactions, avoiding touch, and difficulty understanding the feelings of others. Parents often feel alone and helpless to help their child and face unique stressors. At one time, I was hopeful that "autism awareness" would help people with ASD and their families feel accepted and validated, but over the years I have found that that is not always the case and that in some ways autism awareness has done harm in terms of accepting people and families touched by autism.

My oldest son, now sixteen, is midway on the autism spectrum. I sit here in my blue Autism Awareness Walk T-shirt writing this chapter reflecting on what I initially hoped I would gain by helping to promote autism awareness. I believe I not only hoped for education about autism, but also help, support, and acceptance. And what do I want people to accept? In short, my son's life is hard, his brother's life is hard, my life is hard, and his father's life is hard. It is all hard, day to day and moment to moment. I want when my son has an inevitable meltdown in public, or says socially inappropriate things, and I say to someone watching, "He has autism," they will maybe *maybe* offer some kind of empathic response instead of looking at him and our family with judgment and reproof. Instead, more often than not, people think they know about autism and believe if we were decent people those fits and socially inappropriate remarks would be controlled. This lack of empathy or acceptance of the realities of my own life, I blame, in part, on awareness campaigns.

I was at one time a big supporter of autism awareness. To prove it, I have a blue, stretchy bracelet with the words "Autism Awareness" on it that I initially bought to help spread awareness. And I have a blue stretchy ring. And a key chain shaped like a ribbon made up of puzzle pieces. And several blue T-shirts. And a car magnet shaped like a puzzle. And a refrigerator magnet. Etc. In addition, to spread awareness, I have participated in Autism Awareness Walks and events. Why? Because when my son was diagnosed with autism at the age of five, I considered it my duty to "spread awareness" about autism, partly because the diagnosis was so hard to get and help was difficult to get. In 2001, when my son was born, autism was not in the public consciousness as it is now.

I recall in 2002, a *Time* magazine article caught my attention. The cover featured a boy with his eyes closed and his body in motion as if he were moving to a rhythm that only he could feel. The cover read, "Inside the World of Autism" (May 6, 2002). I don't recall reading the article carefully. It was the cover that struck me, the "in his own world," dreamy, mysterious quality of the boy on the cover. I carried that image with me. Autism began to be mentioned in media, and in 2005, a friend gave me an article in *Newsweek* called "Babies and Autism," saying, "I just felt I should give this to you."

My son was diagnosed with autism in 2006. But when he was born in 2001, autism was not in the public consciousness so much. I spent a lot of time doing my own research as to what was "wrong" with my son who barely spoke. I first told our pediatrician when he was a baby and a toddler that some of his behavior seemed "odd" to me, only to be told that all children develop differently and boys are often "behind" and "hyper." My child did do a lot of things that demonstrated intelligence. But, again, something was amiss and I could not figure it out. I took a list of notes to the doctor on behaviors that seemed to be a problem such as eating things like tissue paper, inability to sit still, lack of following directions, inability to have a conversation, inability to read facial expressions, etc.

I took my son to a noted developmental center in Little Rock, Arkansas, with a list of concerns. After hours testing my child, the team decided that my son was mentally retarded (MR) but I *knew* that was not the case. Days afterward I kept thinking of examples of how intelligent he was. Once, for example, when trying to put up a tent in our backyard, my husband and I could not get the stakes to go into the hard ground so my son went and got a cup of water and poured it on the ground to wet it. That seemed like problem solving to me. He could expertly "drive" the Fisher-Price Jeep we bought to ride around the backyard, avoiding things and animals that were in the way. I argued with the team of people that was telling me he was MR. Realizing that I was having such a hard time with the diagnosis, the doctor recommended that he be seen after a year of intense speech therapy (that insurance did not cover), allowing that his deficits in communication may have impeded his ability to score high on the standardized tests he was orally administered.

After intensive speech therapy, it became apparent that he was not MR but had severe language deficits as well as other problems that are associated with having ASDs such as difficulty taking turns, difficulty reading facial expressions, etc. Once he gained some basic speech and language skills, and MR was ruled out, doctors began to consider autism as a diagnosis. It took me a long time to grapple with the term and what it meant. In spite of all the apprehension I had and the questions I had, I felt a sense of relief in having a name for his behavior. Part of that relief was in being able to tell other people what was "wrong." When he was initially diagnosed, I pictured being able to tell people when he "misbehaved" that "he has autism" and they would understand. And accept both him and our family.

Soon after I got the diagnosis, I began trying to "spread awareness," mainly because it was so hard for me to get a diagnosis and I wanted to get the word out so that people didn't have to live in the dark as I did and could get help earlier. I wanted people to be aware of specific things: that people have autism; that autism is a spectrum ranging from mild to severe; that early detection of autism is important for treatment; that certain treatments exist and some are better than others for certain children; that special education, or certain accommodations, will be necessary for some children; that schools are not always helpful; that people who are supposed to know how to help the child may not be able to or can't for various reasons. I also wanted people to be aware that children with ASD often don't sleep properly. And often don't follow directions. Or often don't talk at all or talk in very limited ways. That they often don't like to be touched. That they often have sensory issues that lead them to sensory overload, leading to tears and fits, etc.

I kept waiting for awareness to lead to acceptance of conditions such as those. But I found, despite awareness, people were not always accepting. And in fact, sometimes, people were the opposite of accepting.

I recall one neighbor who knocked on my door. It was a woman and her friend. When I answered the door, she proceeded to tell me that my child with autism was scaring her daughter because he was carrying a stick and waving it around. This was around the time I would let him play outside with his younger brother. He seemed to need activity and had quit wandering off. I was scared to let him outside, out of my sight, but he seemed to be maturing. I apologized profusely for my child scaring her daughter and said he had problems and autism and I would talk to him and I felt sure it wouldn't happen anymore. She told me that she knew someone with autism and that "there are things you can do." She told me that school counselors could help him. I was in shock. Did she think I didn't seek any help for him? Did she honestly think I wasn't working with the schools and doctors? Did she think that I did not understand my child's condition—that I was "unaware" of it and how to help him? But I politely listened and thanked her since I felt guilty that her daughter was scared and children should not wave around sticks. So, after this initial conversation, she came back again for a reason I cannot even recall, and I, so worried that my child was being a problem affecting others, was apologetic. Until the third time.

It was evening. I was in the backyard watching my child jump on the trampoline. Regardless of his special needs, he is extremely well coordinated, and it was a good way for him to expend excess energy. He saw this neighbor and her children in her own yard and began yelling; it was nothing offensive but I don't recall what he was saying. We went inside after a while and I heard a knock on my door. She, with her children around her, said that my son was yelling at them. At this point, I became upset and told her, "I have told you my child has autism. If all he does is play in his own backyard and yell, I'm happy. I would think other people could deal with it. I take him to a counselor, a psychiatrist, speech therapist, and occupational therapist. I am doing the best I can. Stop acting like I don't know what I'm doing and stop judging him and stop judging me. You are not helpful and I want you to leave and not come back. Why don't you teach your own children some compassion?" Now, could I have handled this better? Probably. However, coping with a child with autism is difficult on a moment-to-moment, day-to-day basis.

Having people be able to empathize with parenting a child with autism or another disability makes a huge difference in a family's ability to cope with the stress and demands of parenting a child on the spectrum. This point of view, taken from my own lived experience, is in keeping with Altiere and von Kluge (2009), who stated, "An individual who provides assistance and understands the child's difficulties makes a significant difference in those [stressful] circumstances" (142). As a parent of a child with autism, I have needed all kinds of social support (informational, instrumental, and emotional) that goes beyond what "normal" parents would need but have not always gotten it. Due to my educational background and tenacity, I have probably coped better than some parents. And, of course, not every interaction has been bad, or everyone unkind, but I think a lot of tears and anxiety could have been saved for me, my family, and ultimately for my child if awareness would have resulted in acceptance and validation of our experience. One problem with awareness campaigns may be that the reality of autism is complex and confusing and people do not like to be confused and prefer a more simple reality.

The parents in the Altiere and von Kluge (2009) article reported feelings of "despair," "depression," being "upset," and "devastated" after their child's diagnosis of autism (145). Parents used words such as "obsessive" and "destructive" to describe their child (145) so much so that one couple had to lock their daughter in a room at night. Indeed, when my son had begun to walk, we closed off our living room and lived in that one room, the four of us, for a year because he would pull down curtains around the house, play with light sockets, pull pictures off the wall, turn over furniture, play in the soil of house plants, climb stairs and over bannisters, and try to get out of the house to the busy street. He climbed over baby gates and knocked them over. Due to this, we eventually moved to a one-level ranch house in a neighborhood with a less busy street and still had to constantly modify our space to make sure he was safe and to preserve the home from destruction. The parents in the Altiere and von Kluge article reported financial, physical, and emotional struggles and stated that their support networks diminished over time so that they did not have "a life" (146). Some reported struggles with family and not being able to attend church due to messages of disapproval of their child's behavior (146). Although some parents reported trying to get others to understand their situation, it took too much time and energy. The parents in the Altiere and von Kluge study did report instances of personal growth and some benefits from parenting a child with autism, but it is obvious the feelings of rejection were overwhelming. Still, Altiere and von Kluge concluded, "It is worthy repeating that families with a child with autism need acceptance and recognition from others" (151).

However, it is not just acceptance from others that parents need to gain. It is acceptance of their own plight. Merely Me, in an article titled "Accepting Your Child's Diagnosis: Are We Going to Holland or Beirut?" (2010) described this process. She noted that parents often find or are given a popular story to read called "Welcome to Holland" by Emily Perl Kingsley (2016), who is a parent of a special needs child. In her story, Kingsley likens raising a special needs child to planning a trip to Italy but winding up in Holland and wrote, "It's just a different place. It's slower-paced than Italy, less flashy than Italy. But after you've been there for a while and you catch your breath, you look around . . . and you begin to notice that Holland has windmills . . . and Holland has tulips. Holland even has Rembrandts." She further stated, "But, if you spend your life mourning the fact that you didn't get to Italy, you may never be free to enjoy the very special, the very lovely things . . . about Holland." Although this story often provides comfort to parents, and indeed it has me, it falls short of capturing the frustration of raising a child with autism for some parents, such as myself. Susan Rzucidl (2016) actually wrote a counter-story entitled "Welcome to Beirut." In it, she wrote:

> There you are in Beirut, dropped in the middle of a war. You don't know the language and you don't know what is going on. Bombs are dropping "Life long diagnosis" and "Neurologically impaired." Bullets whiz by "refrigerator mother" "A good smack is all HE needs to straighten up." Your adrenaline races as the clock ticks away your child's chances for "recovery." You sure as heck didn't sign up for this and want out NOW! God has over estimated your abilities.

Regardless of what inspires or provides comfort, the fact there are stories such as "Welcome to Holland" and "Welcome to Beirut" points to the needs of parents to make sense out of their child's diagnosis and to accept it. During this process, the role of other people can add stress or help alleviate it.

My own feelings of rejection have led me to want to craft a public service advertising campaign of a public service announcement featuring something like a mom and her two small children at a grocery store with a voice-over that says, "See that five-year-old kid making loud noises in the supermarket checkout aisle. . . . ?" The video would show the child picking up candy and unwrapping it while his tired and angry-looking mother picks up his brother's bottle off the floor repeatedly. "That's the twentieth time his mom has picked up his brother's bottle in the store today," the voice-over would continue. Then the mother would say to the five-year-old, "Please just stand quiet. I'll buy you the candy. Don't do this." The child would throw the candy at her and laugh, and the voice-over would say, "Well, I'm sure she doesn't want to pay for the extra candy or have her child eat it in the checkout line, much less have it thrown at her while her child laughs at her for all to see. And I'm sure she is sick of picking up her toddler's bottle at the same time. And I'll bet she wishes she could have left them at home to shop in peace but couldn't for some reason. In fact, I'll bet she wishes she was at home sleeping, along with the kids. . . . Offer acceptance. Not judgment," or something of the kind.

Part of the reason that people lack acceptance is because awareness campaigns have led to the perception that autism is everywhere and have led to two dominant stereotypes of people with autism: an intelligent, peculiar person lacking in social skill and a totally nonverbal person who cannot communicate at all. Both might be true depictions but the middle of the spectrum has been lost. In fact, all people with autism are different and autism is a spectrum disorder. Too many people have heard the term "autism" and at this point are likely to know someone with autism directly or indirectly. A main result of autism awareness campaigns is that now people realize that people have autism. A lot of people have autism, but people may not really know much about it beyond stereotypes and may not be all that accepting of the disorder and the implications of it. So, awareness campaigns have brought autism into the public consciousness. However, acceptance of autism and families touched by autism is still lacking. I believe we are at the point of creating an autism "acceptance" campaign now that people are aware.

Chapter Seven

The Awareness Is Altruistic Myth

Along with raising awareness, the goal of awareness campaigns often includes some element related to fundraising. As seen in the site analysis, sometimes the site or campaign will specify raising money for research to help find a cure for a disease. Other times the use of the money raised will be more vague, such as to help in the fight against a disease. But at any rate, the implication is that with the awareness, the campaign is also doing something by raising money. And money matters, right? In fact, one of the first pushbacks the authors received in discussing the awareness myth with colleagues is that the races and fundraisers and shopping and related activities were, in fact, action.

But beyond the awareness/action debate, there is the issue of how much money is raised, if it is actually raised; how it is used; and perhaps even why. It's called cause marketing. Companies that shroud themselves and their products in pink or other colors of the observation month want consumers to believe they are being good, generous citizens in the fight against some disease. Maybe even your friends and neighbors—maybe even you, and definitely we—have joined in fundraisers such as runs or bake sales in an effort to show support or help the cause.

The fundraising efforts, particularly those tied to corporate sponsorships, associated with the *awareness culture* lead to another myth—the myth that awareness is altruistic. While, as established, the *awareness culture* extends across the landscape of health-related causes, breast cancer awareness is the most visible and therefore has also received the most attention and, frankly, criticism about cause-marketing efforts. As the executive director of the National Women's Health Network, Cindy Pearson, told the *New York Times*, "The pinkification of the month of October, from football cleats to coffee cups, isn't helping women" (Kolata 2015, 9). Similarly, a nurse navigator at a breast imaging center told one of the researchers who was being scheduled for a biopsy, "It makes me angry, too. They just slap a ribbon on [a product] and make money off of it."

A prime, but far from the only, corporate example is the NFL's A Crucial Catch, launched in 2009 in partnership with the American Cancer Society (ACS). For one month in the middle of the football season, professional players are awash in pink from head to toe—in the guise of raising awareness and money to "help fight breast cancer," as featured at nfl.com/pink. With all the exposure and a $7.24 billion industry (Brady 2015) pledging to donate 100 percent of proceeds of Pink October sales to the American Cancer Society, you might assume that would translate into a hefty sum for cancer research. But, it's not the case. First, the "fight" against cancer from NFL support does not go to research. According to VICE Sports:

> This is how it works: The NFL donates proceeds from its awareness campaign, auctions, and the NFL Shop to the American Cancer Society (ACS), which in turns uses that money to increase awareness, education, and screenings for women over 40.
>
> "The money that we receive from NFL has nothing to do with our research program," ACS spokeswoman Tara Peters told VICE Sports. All NFL donations go to ACS' CHANGE program, through which the organization awards grants to "community based health facilities" located within 100 miles of an NFL city for educating women about breast health. The ACS could not provide the names of any of these health facilities, but it says that these centers have answered questions about early detection of the disease for at least 72,000 women in the last three years and screened 10,000 women at little or no cost (Sinha 2014, para 3-4).

Not only is the money raised *not* going to research, the amount of money donated is not what it first seems. While the NFL claims to donate all proceeds of items sold in its shop, that does not translate to a dollar-for-dollar donation because other vendors, distributors, and manufacturers along the chain are not also donating. According to VICE, the only portion going to ACS is the royalty percentage from wholesale sales, which means just a fraction of that $80 hoodie ever made it to help fight breast cancer. "In fact, the NFL's claim of 100 percent proceeds from auction and 100 percent proceeds from retail has translated to an average of just $1.1 million every year since they partnered with ACS six years ago," VICE reported in 2014. "That's less than .01 percent of the approximately $10 billion the league made in revenue last year" (Sinha 2014, para 10).

The NFL's altruism can also be called into question in how it treats players who try to raise awareness on their own. For example, in 2015, the NFL fined DeAngelo Williams $5,757 for wearing eye black that had the breast cancer ribbon and said, "We will find a cure," purportedly for violating uniform policy. A Yahoo sports headline pointed out the irony, "NFL fines DeAngelo Williams for raising breast cancer awareness during breast cancer awareness month." The article noted that in the six years of the Crucial Catch program from 2009 to 2014, the NFL had donated $8 million to the American Cancer Society while fining players $76.8 million (Rohrbach 2015). Williams's altruism, it should be noted, is not being questioned. His mother died from breast cancer in 2014, and in 2015 he donated money to fund fifty-three mammograms in honor of the age of his mother when she died (Fowler 2015).

Williams—with his hair tipped in pink, a gesture he adopted after the NFL refused for him to continue wearing pink after the month of October in 2015—was featured prominently on the NFL's Crucial Catch website, http://www.nfl.com/pink, in the summer of 2016. The site, dominated by pink except for the NFL's red, white, and blue logo over a pink ribbon next to the American Cancer Society's also red, white, and blue logo, trumpeted, "A CRUCIAL CATCH SCREENING SAVES LIVES." While an abundant and growing number of researchers are taking issue with the universal claim that screening saves lives, that discussion is outside the scope of this chapter. Instead, we would simply question that if the NFL truly believes that screening saves lives, why is a relatively paltry percentage going to the cause compared to its profits and even fines against players—as well as why does it fine players for promoting the cause?

The NFL is far from the only corporate sponsor to align with pink awareness campaigns with questionable results if not intentions. In 2015, the *New York Times* headlined, "A Growing Disenchantment with October 'Pinkification.'" The *Times* article cited critics who said breast cancer awareness has become "a sort of feel good catch all associated with screening and early detection, and the ubiquitous pink a marketing opportunity for companies of all type" (Kolata 2015, 5).

As an example, Dick's Sporting Goods has offered free shipping on pink products including football cleats and batting gloves. Its slogan is "Sport your support. Together we'll turn the sports world pink." Yet, as the *Times* article later mentioned, Dick's website indicated, in fine print, that not all of the companies selling the pink products donate money to breast cancer causes. For example, in late August of 2016, the Dick's Breast Cancer Awareness Shop included a pink ribbon with instructions for shoppers to check back in September. In small print with an asterisk, the site said, "*Not all products featured in this collection are subject to a charitable donation." Additionally, some companies have a maximum donation but do not provide a way for customers to know when that cap has been met. So, it could be that none of the money from those pink socks made its way to fight breast cancer in any form.

A primary source for the *New York Times* article about Pinkification was Karuna Jaggar, the executive director of Breast Cancer Action (BCA), an activist group whose slogan is "Think before you pink." BCA published a thirty-page *Think Before You Pink Toolkit* in 2012 that listed several such fundraisers and partnerships and includes questions for consumers to consider.

"We all want to make a difference in the breast cancer epidemic," a section called "Critical Questions for Conscious Consumers" begins. "A lot of companies are selling pink ribbon products that supposedly raise awareness of and money for breast cancer. But did you know that these pink ribbon products may not be making the positive impact the companies claim?" (8). The tool kit included questions to help "conscious consumers . . . make sense of the pink ribbon madness" (8).

The first question was, "Does any money from this purchase go to support breast cancer programs? How much?"

"Any company can put a pink ribbon on its products. The widely recognized pink ribbon symbol is not regulated by any agency and does not necessarily mean it effectively combats the breast cancer epidemic. . . . Can you tell how much money from your purchases will go to support breast cancer programs? If not, consider giving directly to the charity of your choice instead" (BCA 2012, 8).

A 2010 campaign by Dansko shoe was given as an example. The company sold a clog with a pink ribbon and made a $25,000 donation to the Susan G. Komen Foundation. But, no portion of each individual sale was donated.

The second question was, "What organization will get the money? What will they do with the funds, and how do these programs turn the tide of the breast cancer epidemic?" (BCA 2012, 8). It is interesting to note that in our research, along with some resentment of the amount of money raised by and for breast cancer, people involved in other causes also expressed a bit of envy at the number of breast cancer organizations. While there is a range of organizations that support a variety of approaches to fighting, preventing, or ending breast cancer, many other causes are much more limited in their options. For example, a respondent whose mother was diagnosed with early onset Alzheimer's indicated she was not in agreement with the mission of the Alzheimer's Association, but that it was really her only choice in where to contribute. "If you want to help with breast cancer, you have 900 options of where you can give," she said. "But if you want to donate for Alzheimer's, you only have one." So, while the advice of "Think Before You Pink" can be applied to some causes, it's not universal.

The third question was, "Is there a 'cap' on the amount the company will donate? Has this maximum donation already been met? Can you tell?" (BCA 2012, 9):

Some companies that indicate that a portion of the proceeds from the sale of a particular pink ribbon product will go to support breast cancer programs put an arbitrary "cap" on their maximum donation. Once the maximum amount has been met, the company may continue to sell the product with the pink ribbon without alerting customers that no additional funds will be donated to breast cancer organizations. This means you may be buying a product for which none of your purchase price will go to a breast cancer cause but only to the bottom line of the company. (BCA 2012, 9)

Think Before You Pink noted a 2010 Reebok cause-marketing campaign with products featuring pink ribbons. Reebok "heavily promoted" that a portion of its sales would be donated to the Avon Breast Cancer Crusade. However, Reebok set a maximum donation of $750,000 without establishing a way for customers to know if the cap had been met. That meant that while some purchases did in fact result in a donation to the stated cause, others did not. And customers had no way of knowing.

BCA encouraged customers to write companies and ask them to be transparent in their financial contributions as well as to consider giving directly to a breast cancer organization rather than relying on purchased products to support the cause.

Major League Baseball's (MLB) partnership with the Prostate Cancer Foundation (PCF) has not reached the same level of visibility as the NFL's association with breast cancer and thus has not received an equal amount of attention—and criticism. Still, our research, including the case study of the PCF website analyzed in chapter 3, indicated that PCF's and MLB's "Home Run Challenge" was steeped in the *awareness culture* as amusement had crept into donating money to the cancer cause. The MLB logo over the blue ribbon symbolizing prostate cancer awareness that was on the home page of pcf.org was also prominently displayed on the site for the Home Run Challenge at https://homerunchallenge.org. Again, it is beside a photo, or in this case a still shot of a video, of a man recognizable to baseball fans as Hall of Famer Joe Torre. Under the headline "Home Run Challenge" copy said, "Help find a cure for prostate cancer." The site asked visitors to "pledge a donation for every home run hit from June 13 through June 19." June 19 marked Father's Day, on which all teams sported uniforms with blue, the shade of the prostate cancer ribbon. The site gave "STATS" of 2,141 fans donating, $1,762,468 total donations this year, and 241 home runs. A "FAN LEADERBOARD" invited visitors to "see which teams have the most generous fans." The Los Angeles Dodgers were in first place, with seventeen fans donating $32,105.

On the PCF site, a link under "Research News" included the headline "Prostate Cancer Foundation and Major League Baseball Step Up to the Plate to Raise Awareness and Fund Research for Prostate Cancer." The subhead mentioned that the Home Run Challenge was launching "Alongside

New Public Service Announcement by Hall of Famer, MLB Chief Baseball Officer and Prostate Cancer Survivor Joe Torre." The article included links to the homerunchallenge.org website as well as a link to "Celebrate Dad with special MLB commemorative gear and support PCF." The article also announced that royalties from the sale of the specially designed Father's Day uniforms and caps would be donated to PCF. A paragraph about umpires and groundskeepers wearing blue wristbands and blue ribbon uniform decals ended with this sentence: "Major League Baseball Charities has committed $50,000 to PCF as part of this annual effort." The article concluded, "Funding support of the Home Run Challenge by MLB and its Clubs has helped lower the prostate cancer death rate by more than 50 percent and made possible discoveries in prostate cancer that now extend to saving lives in eight other forms of cancer."

As mentioned in chapter 3, although prostate cancer affects men at roughly the same rate, one in eight, as breast cancer does women, prostate cancer awareness has not reached anywhere near the same level of visibility as breast cancer awareness. Perhaps that's one reason why the PCF and MLB partnership has not had the same level of scrutiny and criticism as the NFL's Crucial Catch campaign for breast cancer. Our Internet searches for PCF, MLB, and Home Run Challenge resulted in no negative reports on the first page of links as similar searches related to breast cancer have. In other words, there is no parallel "Review Before You Blue" like there is a "Think Before You Pink." If the Think Before You Pink framework were applied to the Home Run Challenge, however, we think there would be some similarities. As a prime example, MLB itself pledged a set amount of $50,000 for the 2016 challenge. In contrast, *Forbes* reported the MLB baseball revenues at more than $9 billion in 2015 (Brown 2015). Beyond the $50,000, donations were from fans who pledged money for each home run hit by their selected team for a week. It's true that fans could also give a set donation, but the entire structure of the challenge was based on one team outslugging another. If the goal was to cure prostate cancer, why not simply donate rather than waiting to see if a player likely making millions of dollars a year hits a ball over a wall? Why must it be a game or a spectacle if the donation is altruistic?

Breast and prostate cancer are not the only examples of awareness campaigns with controversial fundraising techniques. Perhaps the most prolific awareness campaign in recent years has been the Ice Bucket Challenge to raise awareness and money for the ALS Association (ALSA). As discussed in more detail previously, the Ice Bucket Challenge, also sometimes called the ALS Ice Bucket Challenge, was a viral phenomenon in summer of 2014 that raised over $100 million for ALSA. The idea behind the challenge was that participants were challenged to dump water on their heads or make a donation to ALSA. After posting their version of being soaked in ice water, the participant would then challenge five more people to participate. In terms of sheer numbers, the Ice Bucket Challenge was an unqualified success. *Time* called it a "break-the-Internet phenomenon that spread all the way up to President Obama" in raising $115 million for ALSA. In contrast, ALSA reported $23.5 million in donations in the previous year.

In somewhat of a twist, the ALS Ice Bucket Challenge participants were taking action by dumping water and raising money, but there was still skepticism about the meaning and motivation of the challenge. As Wolff-Mann of *Time* asked, "Was the campaign saying it was better to be cold and wet than a charitable giver?" (Wolff-Mann 2015, 2). A common criticism was that participants were more interested in being part of a fad than actually learning about the disease or how to help those suffering from it. During the campaign, various people raised concerns that participants were more caught up in the viral sensation than the cause, giving less money than a typical donor and often without even knowing much about the disease. The *Time* article quoted Tim Gamory, the acting COO of Charity Navigator, who praised the transparency of ALSA but also questioned the motivation of participants: "'Some people didn't even know about ALS—it just became Ice Bucket Challenge,' said Gamory. 'So it would be interesting to see data as far as what people actually know. I can tell you from our site, the searches for ALS went up a ridiculous amount, from around 500 to 68,000 in August. And then it went right back down'" (Woff-Mann 2015, 12).

The *Time* article noted a difference in sustained donors and those who "respond to the social media wave" (Wolff-Mann 2015, 14) in a form of slacktivism. "'As far as any longer term impact on those donor people who were exposed, it's questionable,' said Gamory. 'Many of the donors were flash-in-the-pan'" (Wolff-Mann 2015, 14). Additionally, according to other media outlets, only a fraction of participants actually donated. The BBC reported that one in ten people who took the challenge actually donated to ALSA. Awareness? Perhaps, if unlikely. Altruism? Most likely not.

ALSA attempted a second social media wave of the Ice Bucket Challenge in 2015 with the slogan "Every August Until a Cure" and again in 2016 with "Every Drop Adds Up." The subsequent installments did not have the same level of viral success but did face critics. The ALSA Facebook page was peppered with comments questioning the challenge. The criticisms ranged from protesting wasted water to how the money raised in 2014 was used. "I just don't understand why people waste water to donate money??!!" one person asked. Another added, "How does dumping ice water on yourself actually contribute to science? Those people were just going along with social media's bandwagon. Donate money or volunteer your time. Be useful." Still another, "So many people donated an incredible amount of money to ALS. More money that they could imagine but somehow this isn't enough? They want more now? Are you kidding me? Keep donating until a cure? What's the point of the cure if the millions keep pouring in? What a bunch of crooks." One 2015 commenter succinctly summed up the flash-in-the-pan phenomenon "This is so last year."

Reporting the criticism is not to say that no good came from the challenge. *Time* (Wolff-Mann 2015) reported that Charity Navigator "commended" ALSA on its use of the funds. Additionally, family members of those with ALS left comments about help they received from the charity. As Wolff-Mann said, "Even if most donors don't know what the letters 'ALS' stand for or anything about the illness, it's hard to look a $115 million gift horse in the mouth" (Wolff-Mann 2015, 15).

The leaders at BCA might or might not agree. The *Think Before You Pink Toolkit* included a discussion on breast cancer runs and walks. The toolkit acknowledged the "personal commitment, passion, and camaraderie involved" and noted that "walks and runs can be a terrific opportunity to connect with others and feel less alone in one's cancer experience" (BCA 2012, 10). Still, the BCA expressed concern that the walks and runs primarily functioned to raise money for breast cancer. Specific points of concern were inefficiency, lack of transparency, doubts about awareness, diverted resources, and ties to pinkwashing.

Inefficiency—More than half of the money raised by participants goes to support the event itself (BCA 2012).

Lack of transparency—The actual purpose of the event and final destination of funds raised is not immediately clear. "'Awareness' is one of the most common aims of these walks. While we are all aware breast cancer is a problem, too little funding goes to addressing the root causes of the epidemic" (BCA 2012, 10).

Doubts about awareness—There are increasing questions about the role of "awareness" and who it benefits:

> Although organizers and participants claim these events raise awareness, most people involved acknowledge that sponsors are supporting the individual person rather than demonstrating and deepening their concern about breast cancer. Furthermore, there are questions about what kind of awareness is raised. Do these walks educate people about the surprising facts and ugly truths of breast cancer? Do they further the growing perception that breast cancer has too much of the limelight while other diseases need more funding? (BCA 2012, 10).

Diverted resources—The time, money, energy, and other resources spent on races/walks are not always the best return on investment. BCA would like to see those resources funneled to uprooting the causes of breast cancer.

Ties to pinkwashing—Some corporations sponsor runs/walks as a method of cause marketing, but their products are not safe. As an example, BCA referenced Avon, which includes parabens and pthalates in some cosmetics, chemicals that have been linked to breast cancer.

Taken together, BCA has come out against cause-related events, even if seemingly well-intentioned. "For these reasons, BCAction believes there are more effective ways to address the breast cancer epidemic than participating in a walk or run" (2012, 10).

It is not just corporations engaging in cause marketing that are selling products as fundraisers. As the analysis in chapter 3 demonstrated, websites of some awareness organizations themselves are awash with products featuring logos and ribbons. More than half featured a "shop" or "store" button, some multiple times. For example, the top of the home page of the National Breast Cancer Foundation (NBCF) included a "shop" button. Clicking on the button led to a page that said, "Share Hope with Friends." Products ranged from a $2 wristband to a $40 polo shirt. The website said, "The NBCF shop is full of gifts that offer hope with 100 percent of net proceeds benefiting programs which are Helping Women Now®."

The shop page at autismspeaks.org featured a range of blue products, including "Mellow the Different Not Less Dino" for $24.95 and an "Autism Speaks Cotton Lounge Pant" for $20.99. The site specified that "autism awareness products, autism shirts, and autism awareness day gifts" could be found at Shop.AustimSpeaks.org. The organization added in a section called "Autism Awareness Products" that buying from the site would support its mission. "Each purchase on Shop.AutismSpeaks.org allows Autism Speaks to continue its search for the causes and most effective treatments for autism and provide information, tools, and resources to improve the lives of individuals and families affected by autism," shop.autismspeaks.org said.

The American Childhood Cancer Organization online store featured more relatable products ranging from Hero Beads, to a stuffed animal, and survivor pins and charms. There was also a specific section for "ACCO Awareness Items" listing more than twenty products from 75-cent silicone bracelets to a $2.50 pair of shoelaces and a $40 "Family Pack Awareness Kit." The site said, "American Childhood Cancer Organization is a 501(c)(3) charitable organization. All proceeds from our web store support ACCO's free resources for children with cancer and their families." The ACCO site seemed less commercial in some ways than other sites—as if the products were resources for those affected with childhood cancer. Plus, the site said proceeds support "free resources for children with cancer and their families." So, while the families or those affected might be paying for the products, the money goes back to provide resources to others. Perhaps it is not exactly altruistic, but it doesn't seem as commercialized or faddish either. Additionally, a partner selling hats on the site also provided free hats to "child or teen cancer warrior(s)."

Beyond our original analysis, a quick scan showed that the shopping phenomenon is not limited to our case studies. The Susan G. Komen website included a link to ShopKomen.com, which advertised, "Shop now and help end breast cancer forever." The online store included dozens of products, including a black backpack for $88.75 that includes a pink ribbon and Susan G. Komen logo. The American Heart Association has a HeartShop website featuring Go Red products. The Alzheimer's Association "shop for the cause" has "Alzheimer and Brain Awareness Month" items such as #ENDALZ Striped Tube Socks for $6.99, Alzheimer's Association Neckties for $24.99, and men's and women's Alzheimer's Association Purple Dress Shirts for $36.99. The http://shop.alz.org/ says, "Wear Purple. Raise Awareness. Shop now."

With some sites explicitly stating that proceeds support the cause, there could be an understandable tendency to think that support through shopping is overall positive. And, in some instances, we would agree. Or more specifically, we can see that in instances such as childhood cancer, there is a need for products to support families directly affected. And, we can see that the proceeds all go directly to the cause. But, not all products or organization stores are as directly linked with the causes they support.

For example, BCA addressed the frequently asked question "Isn't any money for breast cancer good?" with a resounding "No." The central issue is that the pink ribbon symbolizing breast cancer awareness is not regulated. Companies can stamp the logo on any sort of products as an attempt to brand themselves as supporting the fight against breast cancer. In truth, a percentage of money might go to a breast cancer organization, or the company could simply be promoting awareness. There's no immediate way to tell. "Because the pink ribbon is not regulated, consumers must look beyond the ribbon to know what is actually going on" (BCA 2012, 12). (It should be noted that Komen has trademarked its pink "running ribbon" at least in part to address this issue.)

BCA also does not believe companies are above criticism simply because they have donated some money. The organization expressed a concern that people are spending money on products with pink ribbons because they think these purchases will somehow help end breast cancer, when in reality there is no guarantee where the money goes, and the money that is funneled to a breast cancer organization often goes for awareness and not prevention. BCA continued,

> The worst part of pink ribbon marketing is "pinkwashers," or companies or organizations claiming to care about breast cancer by promoting a pink ribbon product, but at the same time producing, manufacturing, and/or selling products that are linked to the disease. Companies are profiting from a disease they help create, and we think women deserve better. (BCA 2012, 12)

Finally, BCA disagrees that companies should be applauded for what contributions are made. "'Better than doing nothing' is not good enough," the *toolkit* said (BCA 2012, 12). In fact, BCA sees the cause marketing and donations as counterproductive to effective action:

> We think the huge amount of pink ribbon fundraising allows people to think the problem is taken care of when in fact the problem is not any closer to being solved. As long as consumers think they're doing something meaningful about breast cancer by participating in cause-related marketing campaigns, the real work that needs to be done around treatment, access to care, and true prevention will continue to be underfunded and ignored. In effect, pink ribbon fundraising is diverting and pacifying the public into thinking we are addressing breast cancer issues while issues of prevention are ignored. (2012, 12)

In interviews and field notes, many people acknowledged that they had donated or supported a cause because it is the socially acceptable thing to do. The need to "do something" was one reason for giving. A frequent 5K runner noted that she preferred to participate in races that supported community causes as opposed to for-profit or national organizations. Respondents gave other, less flattering, reasons for why people might donate through sponsorships or buy cause-branded product often displaying ribbons, such as assuaging guilt, self-righteousness, or self-indulgence in the case of fads or trends like the ALS Ice Bucket Challenge. Respondents expressed disapproval yet also a sense of resignation of what one described as a "spectacle." For example, they took issue with organizations that give to causes within a preset budget but also look to *make* money from the sponsorship through a cause-marketing effort, such as selling a product featuring a ribbon related to a health cause or campaign. Additionally, a respondent pointed out that vendors at places like fairs can move merchandise by placing ribbons—particularly pink—on products like purses and belts without making any claim that any proceeds will go to support a cause. This begs the question of what the symbol is supporting.

In short, whether through donations based on cause marketing by companies, purchases of products from awareness organizations, or participation in fundraisers such as challenges, races, or walks, awareness is not altruistic. It's not even particularly effective and could be counter productive by siphoning resources from prevention and research leading to cures. As BCA's Jagger told VICE concerning the NFL's pink campaign, "You can't shop your way out of the breast cancer epidemic" (Sinha 2014, 11). And, we would add, or anything else.

Chapter Eight

The Awareness Equals Health Myth

Implicit in awareness campaigns and the *awareness culture* seems to be the idea that being aware leads to improved health or even a state of wellness. It just makes sense, right? If you're aware that there is an issue, you can avoid or at least improve it? For example, the U.S. Department of Health and Human Services in 2016 included toolkits to "help you make a difference" on a website of National Health Observances dedicated "to raising awareness about important health topics." There is an implied endorsement from the U.S. Department of Health and Human Services that raising awareness does in fact lead to improved health. The resources of the federal government, after all, were supporting toolkits to increase awareness.

However, our primary research supported something secondary research had indicated: the idea that awareness equals health is a myth. In fact, we were struck by the term "sociological placebo" used to describe awareness campaigns in a conversation about the *awareness culture*. "I think with awareness campaigns, most people know deep down that they don't do what they are supposed to, like a sociological placebo," one respondent explained, "but the pressure to appear good to the rest of society gives things like awareness campaigns a life span way longer than they should get."

We identified three primary reasons that the *awareness culture* leads to the Awareness Equals Health Myth:

1) Awareness campaigns do not always provide helpful or beneficial information—and in fact can sometimes include detrimental elements,

2) Evidence suggests that awareness is not effective in leading to a change in behavior or lifestyle, and

3) Increased awareness can actually make behavior appear "normal" and therefore lead to increased unhealthy behavior.

Reason #1—Awareness Equals Health Myth: Awareness campaigns don't always provide helpful or beneficial information and in fact can sometimes be detrimental.

Some awareness campaigns don't promote healthier lifestyles or preventative measures but actually include features that could be detrimental to improved wellness. As found in the analysis of websites, the *awareness culture* is steeped in an emphasis on shopping, sponsors, observation and events, and finding cures and treatments rather than prevention. Only the Prostate Cancer Foundation at www.pcf.org even mentioned nutrition. Looking at missions listed on the web pages as well as the U.S. Health and Human Services site, we did not find evidence that a primary concern of the health-related organizations was actually promoting healthy lifestyles. While the sites mentioned resources and references to research, there were seldom clear steps or recommendations to prevent or lower the risk of a disease, when possible. Again, it seems that by the very fact people had visited the site awareness had already been accomplished and instead causes should focus on how-to knowledge or steps toward implementing beneficial or preventative action, but these steps were not evident.

The vast majority of attention about the subject of awareness campaigns has been breast cancer. We commend and recommend *Pink Ribbons, Inc.* (King 2006); *Pink Ribbon Blues: How Breast Cancer Culture Undermines Women's Health* (Sulik 2012); and *Unnatural History: Breast Cancer and American Society* (Aronowitz 2007) for a thorough examination of the impact and unintended consequences breast cancer awareness campaigns have had specifically on women's health and more broadly on American culture. We also, quite frankly, are a bit surprised that given the information provided in these books as well as advocacy by groups such as Breast Cancer Action (BCA) plus coverage in mainstream media such as the *New York Times* the breast cancer awareness observances continue unabated throughout October—or what BCA called "National Breast Cancer Industry Month." For example, in 2015, the *New York Times* published a story headlined "A Growing Disenchantment with October 'Pinkification'" that quoted a women's health advocate on the limitations of the pink movement. "'The pinkification of the month of October, from football cleats to coffee cups, isn't helping women,' said Cindy Pearson, the executive director of the National Women's Health Network, an advocacy organization," the *Times* wrote (Kolata 2015, para 9).

Another pink-related term is "pinkwashing," which BCA coined in conjunction with its Think Before You Pink campaign. BCA described "pinkwashing" as "a company or organization that claims to care about breast cancer by promoting a pink ribbon product, but at the same time produces, manufactures and/or sells products that are linked to the disease," (BCA 2012, para 1). BCA published *Think Before You Pink Toolkit* and noted:

Over the past 10 years, Think Before You Pink® has changed the conversation around breast cancer cause marketing. The term "pinkwasher" is now a common term used freely by many advocacy organizations and the media to describe the hypocrisy and lack of transparency that surrounds breast cancer fundraising and Breast Cancer Awareness Month. Think Before You Pink® campaigns have successfully targeted cosmetic giant Avon; car manufacturers Ford, Mercedes, and BMW; and Yoplait yogurt maker General Mills. (BCA 2012, para 1)

While there are a growing number of voices questioning all things pink and we definitely applaud the efforts of BCA, National Breast Cancer Awareness Month (NBCAM) in October still remains a powerful cause marketing force generating questionable information associated with breast cancer. We reference extensively from BCA's toolkit to address the myth that Awareness Equals Health:

> However, the corporate takeover of the pink ribbon has so narrowly focused popular attention on awareness that prevention continues to be overlooked. (BCA 2012, 2)
> Pink ribbons have become a distraction. They divert our attention away from the root causes of this disease. Pink ribbons politely ask us to spend our money on many products that may increase our risk of developing breast cancer. For the sake of all our lives, we must do more than shop (and walk and run), because despite our best intentions, these acts have not brought an end to this epidemic. (BCA 2012, 3)

From the start, the pink ribbon campaigns co-opted efforts to promote prevention. According to BCA (and as covered in Unit 1), in the early 1990s Charlotte Haley sent postcards with peach-colored ribbons in an effort to try to get more federal funding for cancer prevention. The cards read, "The National Cancer Institute's annual budget is $1.8 billion, only 5 percent goes for cancer prevention. Help us wake up our legislators and America by wearing this ribbon" (King 2006, xxiv). *Self* magazine and Estee Lauder saw the potential of the ribbon campaign and requested to use it, but Haley found their proposals too commercial and declined. After consulting with attorneys and focus group research, *Self* and Estee Lauder chose the pink ribbon as a symbol for Breast Cancer Awareness Month promotions (King 2006).

There have been advances, to be sure, including increased insurance coverage for mammograms. Of all the benefits of the breast cancer awareness campaigns, decreased stigmatism could be the most meaningful. Billions of dollars have been spent on awareness campaigns along with research and even screenings, but breast cancer is still prevalent. BCA asked why, and then answered it was because the focus was on profits rather than prevention for many of the corporations who promote pink ribbons. Not promoting prevention is one thing, but BCA and other advocacy groups have taken the accusation further, saying that, in fact, some of the companies that are involved in awareness campaigns and fundraisers are actually profiting from products that have been associated with cancer:

> Many companies have sold pink ribbon products that are linked to increased risk of breast cancer. We believe that companies that are profiting from building a reputation based on their concern about breast cancer have a responsibility to protect the public from possible harms when scientific research indicates that there is a risk or plausible reason for concern. Some of the earliest cause-marketing companies were well-known cosmetics companies that continue to sell cosmetics containing chemicals that have been linked to breast cancer. (BCA 2012, 9)

We join with those asking for consumers who desire to help fight breast cancer to look below the pink surface. As the *Think Before You Pink Toolkit* emphasized, the idea is to curtail pinkwashing by ensuring that purchasing a pink-laced product presumably in the fight against breast cancer does not actually lead to an increased risk of cancer. A critical question for "conscious consumers" to ask is, "Does this purchase put you or someone you love at risk for exposure to toxins linked to breast cancer? What is the company doing to ensure that its products are not contributing to the breast cancer epidemic?" (BCA 2012, 9). The possibility that pink products could actually increase the risk of breast cancer is just one way that the idea awareness equals health is a myth.

BCA is not the only group questioning the events surrounding NBCAM, and pink products are not the only potential risk factor to women's health. In 2013, the *New York Times* ran a story called "Our Feel-Good War on Breast Cancer" (Orenstein). The goal of many breast cancer awareness campaigns seems to be to encourage women to get regular screening mammograms, yet the *New York Times* cited a study published in the *New England Journal of Medicine* that questioned the prevailing status of mammograms as improving women's health and saving lives:

> Recently, a survey of three decades of screening published in November in *The New England Journal of Medicine* found that mammography's impact is decidedly mixed: it does reduce, by a small percentage, the number of women who are told they have late-stage cancer, but it is far more likely to result in overdiagnosis and unnecessary treatment, including surgery, weeks of radiation and potentially toxic drugs. And yet, mammography remains an unquestioned pillar of the pink-ribbon awareness movement. Just about everywhere I go—the supermarket, the dry cleaner, the gym, the gas pump, the movie theater, the airport, the florist, the bank, the mall—I see posters proclaiming that "early detection is the best protection" and "mammograms save lives." But how many lives, exactly, are being "saved," under what circumstances and at what cost? Raising the public profile of breast cancer, a disease once spoken of

only in whispers, was at one time critically important, as was emphasizing the benefits of screening. But there are unintended consequences to ever-greater "awareness"—and they, too, affect women's health. (Orenstein 2013, para 6)

We use breast cancer, again, as the most visible example and add our voices to those calling for campaigns to promote health beyond awareness observances. As the breast cancer example has shown, increased corporate sponsorship can come with a cost, and screenings may not be a cure-all. A fuller discussion, in fact, of the limitations and potential risks of screenings is included later in this chapter. For those reasons, other health-related organizations are well advised *not* to model themselves after breast cancer.

Reason #2—Awareness Equals Health Myth: Awareness is not effective in leading to a change in behavior or lifestyle.

Of course, providing meaningful information is also no magic bullet for awareness campaigns. In terms of the extent that awareness leads to a change in behavior or lifestyle, behavioral change theories have proven important in developing successful health promotion activities—and also provide context for the limitations of the *awareness culture.* Korda and Itani (2013) noted previous studies about behavioral change theory and techniques in their article "Harnessing Social Media for Health Promotion and Behavior Change." One of the most comprehensive investigations, a meta-analysis of eighty-five studies by Webb et al. (2010), included a sample size of more than 42,000 participants that had been part of interventions that were delivered primarily via the Internet. The study found that being strongly grounded in theory was associated with interventions having greater impact than non-theory-based interventions. Additionally, "interventions that incorporated more behavior change techniques tended to have larger effects than interventions that incorporated fewer techniques" (Webb et al. 2010, 5). Korda and Itani (2013) highlighted the disconnect between scholarship on the benefits of theory-based approaches and the actual current practices. "These findings underscore the importance of using a validated theoretical framework as a road map for program design and development. Still, many health behavior change websites are not theory driven and fail to incorporate proven, evidence-based approaches" (Korda and Itani 2013, 19). For example, in a review of almost forty sites dedicated to public health and behavior change, Evers et al. (2003) found that few were rooted in evidence-based approaches or theory.

Samantha King (2006) authored a critique of the approach of breast cancer awareness efforts, citing evidence that the events distracted from research aimed at finding out what causes breast cancer and how it might be prevented. King, an associate professor of kinesiology and health at Queen's University in Ontario at the time of the writing, was also quoted in the *New York*

Times article "Our Feel-Good War on Breast Cancer" about the disconnect of awareness campaigns with research:

> "These campaigns all have a similar superficiality in terms of the response they require from the public," King said. "They're divorced from any critique of health care policy or the politics of funding biomedical research. They reinforce a single-issue competitive model of fund-raising. And they whitewash illness: we're made 'aware' of a disease yet totally removed from the challenging and often devastating realities of its sufferers." (Orenstein 2013, para. 40)

New York Magazine addressed the futility of awareness campaigns in a 2014 article headlined "Awareness Is Overrated" (Singal 2014). Singal (2014) referenced the "golden age of awareness-raising" (para 2) then added that the awareness efforts were not actually effective. "The underlying assumption of so many attempts to influence people's behavior—that they make bad choices because they lack the information to empower them to do otherwise—is, except in a few cases, false," Singal wrote. "And what's worse, awareness-raising done in the wrong way can actually backfire, encouraging the negative activities in question" (Singal 2014, para 3).

A primary source for the Singal (2014) article was Victor Strecher with the University of Michigan's School of Public Health. Strecher and colleagues have studied the effectiveness of health campaigns in achieving behavior change for three decades, including the role of self-efficacy (Strecher, DeVellis, Becker, and Rosenstock 1986).

"We've known for over 50 years that providing information alone to people does not change their behavior," Strecher told *New York Magazine*. "It's something of a consensus among people who study behavioral interventions ranging from health to bullying to crime: There are a lot of reasons why people do what they do, but a lack of awareness of their actions' potential repercussions ranks pretty far down the list" (Singal 2014, para 4).

Singal (2014) noted the "rapidly diminishing returns" of raising awareness once a benchmark level of awareness has been reached. Additionally, the "knowledge deficit" isn't the most likely culprit when people engage in actions that are detrimental to their health. Instead of ever-increasing awareness, successful campaigns are based on rigorous work and research:

> What all these effective behavioral-intervention methods have in common is that they attack the roots of people's behaviors in sophisticated ways, and as a result, they take a fair amount of effort to develop. Awareness-raising, on the other hand, is easier and more straightforward, and this can help explain why it's so prevalent despite the dearth of empirical evidence it works. Activists and politicians and public-health officials are just as susceptible to cognitive miserliness as everyone else—they'll often get nudged down the path of least resistance toward awareness-raising rather than carefully and empirically eval-

uate what works and what doesn't. (It doesn't hurt that it's often easier to take credit for a splashy PSA campaign than for more under-the-radar interventions). (Singal 2014, para 23)

In addition to not applying research about how knowledge affects behavior change, the splashy campaigns also do not take into account scholarship about the benefits of targeting specific publics. For example, Hawkins et al. (2008) studied how tailoring individualized messages can improve both cognitive message processing as well as the impact of the message. By creating blanket, one-size-fits-all campaigns rather than tailoring messages designed to address specific groups, communicators are missing opportunities to apply known scholarship about the most effective communication strategies and thus missing opportunities to actually change behaviors that might in fact lead to improved health.

Harold Pollack with the University of Chicago School of Social Service Administration has studied behavior change strategies and health-related issues such as childhood obesity, substance abuse, and smoking cessation and agrees with the benefits of tailoring messages. According to Pollack, "In each context we have to be evidence-based and look [and] see what works, because for different groups of people, different things will work" (Singal 2014, para 12). Part of what has been found to be effective is a "surgical approach" of targeting groups and using a form of positive peer pressure. "Another big focal point of successful behavioral interventions is social norms, which can be a powerful tool when wielded correctly." (Singal 2014, para 17)

Reason #3—Awareness Equals Health Myth: Awareness normalizes and reinforces unhealthy or destructive behaviors.

Social norms can no doubt be a positive force, but research also shows that increased awareness can have a detrimental effect by making behavior appear "normal" and therefore lead to increased unhealthy behavior. In normalizing the behavior that health campaigns want to change, awareness is not just overrated but also counterproductive. "In the most unfortunate cases, raising awareness can have the opposite of its intended effect" (Singal 2014, para 6).

Perhaps slightly outside health causes but still instructive about awareness campaigns are lessons learned from sexual assault education programs in higher education. A *U.S. News & World Report* article, "Campus Sexual Assault: More Awareness Hasn't Solved Root Issues," summarized the efforts of a federal initiative called "It's on Us" to address sexual assault in colleges and universities (Bidwell 2015). The federal grants resulted in more education and training, but the article cited the White House's own task force report about research that has shown the lack of effectiveness of awareness campaigns in changing behavior over the long-term. Bidwell (2015) also quoted Wendy Murphy, an adjunct faculty member at the New England School of Law who has published research on sexual assault and victim advocacy:

> "What some studies show is training and education programs help students who will choose to do the wrong thing . . . learn how to do it without getting caught," Murphy says. "Sometimes too much training about where the lines are and what behavior is acceptable and what isn't really becomes a source of legitimacy around the bad behavior because you're really teaching people that so long as you don't go over this line you can do very bad things." (Bidwell 2015, para 11)

SURVIVORS AND SCREENINGS

Taken together, the lack of beneficial information in awareness campaigns, the questionable impact of knowledge to change behavior, and the possible reinforcement of detrimental lifestyles based on social norms point to the myth that Awareness Equals Health. For a time, the working title of this chapter was "The Awareness Saves Lives Myth." Despite some of the evidence from previous studies as well as current research, we were uncomfortable with saying that awareness saves lives is a myth. Perhaps it was because we didn't want to seem *that* negative. Perhaps it was out of respect for friends and colleagues who have survived breast cancer and wear pink ribbons and participate in Walks for the Cure. Perhaps it was not to tempt fate. Ultimately, there was enough evidence and even personal experience that in some cases awareness *has* saved lives—such as in the explanation of what awareness means to the mother of a baby girl who was diagnosed with cancer. Still, it is worth noting that in discussions about how the events and activities surrounding awareness campaigns seem to promote health but don't actually lead to healthier lifestyles—and in some instances such as ALS there is not anything that we even know we can do to prevent the disease—our research assistant said, "You know, it seems what you are saying is that it's a myth that awareness saves lives."

As hard as it is to hear, there is some truth in that statement—at least on some levels and for some causes. Again, breast cancer has received the most attention and is thus the most visible example. Reading Samantha King's ethnography of a Race for the Cure event made the realization undeniable. King (2006) described the breast cancer survivors participating in the event as "proud, vibrant, hopeful, and passionate, clad in brightly colored athletic apparel, and participating in a vigorous physical activity to raise money for a worthy cause" (35). The description noted the contrast to the "weak, pale, bedridden, cancer victim" of prior decades, most especially documented by Audre Lorde in *Cancer Journal*. Observing the vitality of the survivor celebration at the Race for the Cure, King (2006) noted, "The resulting rhetoric is so upbeat and so optimistic that it is possible to deduce from these events that breast cancer is a curable disease from which people no longer die" (36).

But people—men and women—do die of breast cancer. Breast cancer IS a killer, and the survival stories matter and make the fight relevant. But it's also true that there are different types of breast cancer, and not all women with breast cancer feel welcome at the survival celebrations. The truth is some breast cancer is terminal. What are women—and men—dying of breast cancer to do at a survival rally?

Both *Pink Ribbons, Inc.* (King 2006) and *Pink Ribbon Blues: How Breast Cancer Culture Undermines Women's Health* by Gayle Sulik (2012) are worth reading for a fuller explanation of the implications of America's approach to breast cancer. In fact, the title of Sulik's book points squarely at the myth of Awareness Equals Health. Sulik (2012) gave an in-depth accounting of how the "pink ribbon culture" as a system took attention away from more effective approaches to breast cancer. The distractions range from an overemphasis on screening to the portrayal of women with breast cancer, particularly survivors. Writing about the emphasis on mammograms, Sulik (2012) wrote, "[T]he increase in early-stage diagnoses does not translate to a corresponding decline in late-stage cancers, as would be expected if early detection were successful in preventing the development of more advanced (and less curable) cancers later on" (11). Additionally, she listed the disconnect between the "imagery of millions of participants who walk or run for a cure every year donning smiling faces and pink paraphernalia" (12) and the reality of cancer as part of the pink ribbon culture that has "impeded progress in the war on breast cancer" (12).

In particular, Sulik (2012) highlighted the portrayal of "survivors." She cited Barbara Ehrenreich in referencing "the mandate to be cheerful as a form of tyranny that can take women unawares when facing what is cast as, and what may be, mortal danger" (17). Women with breast cancer who "publicly claim triumphant survivorship" (Sulik 2012, 234) are lauded by the culture that will "marginalize those who do not passionately participate and cheerfully comply with the culture's rules of survivorship" (Sulik 2012, 274). As Orenstein (2013) wrote in "Our Feel-Good War on Breast Cancer," published in the *New York Times*, "Perhaps for that reason, metastatic patients are notably absent from pink-ribbon campaigns, rarely on the speaker's podium at fund-raisers or races" (para. 55).

But, looking strong and vibrant—like the picture of health, in other words—does not correlate to actually being healthy. An analysis of the National Breast Cancer Foundation site supported the myth that Awareness Equals Health. As mentioned in chapter 3, the site was full of hope and hype. Pictures were overwhelmingly of smiling people and survivors. Even the photograph of metastatic breast cancer retreat included the headline "restoring hope." The influence of the pink ribbon culture in spreading to other causes and creating an *awareness culture* was also seen in the Prostate Cancer Foundation website, which featured athletic imagery.

The influence of breast cancer culture on the approach to other cancers, particularly prostate, can largely be seen in the emphasis on screening with little discussion of contradictory evidence. It is somewhat surprising, for example, to learn that in 2009 the American Cancer Society acknowledged the limits of screening to the *New York Times*. "We don't want people to panic," said Dr. Otis Brawley, chief medical officer of the cancer society. "But I'm admitting that American medicine has overpromised when it comes to screening. The advantages to screening have been exaggerated" (Kolak 2009, para 3). The headline—"Cancer Society, in Shift, Has Concerns on Screenings"—and lead—"The American Cancer Society, which has long been a staunch defender of most cancer screening, is now saying that the benefits of detecting many cancers, especially breast and prostate, have been overstated" (Kolata 2009, para 1)—were clear and undeniable. The article stated that ACS was planning to publish a statement on its website to "emphasize that screening for breast and prostate cancer and certain other cancers can come with a real risk of overtreating many small cancers while missing cancers that are deadly" (Kolata 2009, para 2). Yet, the call for screenings in awareness efforts and observances has remained largely unabated—if not grown.

Orenstein's 2013 article, "Our Feel-Good War on Breast Cancer," went into somewhat troubling detail about the lack of consistency in what research has shown to be the mixed results and limitations of screenings and the continued reliance on mammography without consideration for potential adverse effects. A quotation previously included as evidence of the detrimental effects of some awareness messages is worth repeating here: "[M]ammography remains an unquestioned pillar of the pink-ribbon awareness movement. . . . But there are unintended consequences to ever-greater 'awareness'—and they, too, affect women's health" (Orenstein 2013, para 7).

Awareness campaigns were successful in terms of the number of people who went for screenings as well as an increase in the number of cancers found and the survival of patients following initial treatments. However, there were limits to the success. "[T]he rates of women dying of breast cancer hardly budged. All those increased diagnoses were not translating into 'saved lives.' That should have been a sign that some aspect of the early-detection theory was amiss. Instead, surgeons believed they just needed to find the disease even sooner" (Orenstein 2013, para 10).

More than discussing the limits of mammography, Orenstein (2013) also pointed out that the emphasis on screening was detrimental. For one, there was evidence through surveys that some women misunderstood the purpose of mammograms and thought the screenings could prevent rather than simply detect cancer. Even more directly related to the Awareness Equals Health Myth, awareness campaigns had ironically, like Sulik (2012) said in her book, undermined women's health. "Yet all that well-meaning awareness has ultimately made women *less* conscious of the facts: obscuring the limits of screening, conflating risk with disease, compromising our decisions about health care, celebrating 'cancer survivors' who may have never required treating. And ultimately, it has come at the expense of those whose lives are most at risk" (Orenstein 2013, para 59).

Breast cancer is not the only disease in which the benefits of screening have been exaggerated while the possible consequences have been minimized. As mentioned earlier, screening for prostate cancer, too, was mentioned by the American Cancer Society as a case where the benefits were "overstated." In a special to CNN, ACS's Bawley "expressed concern about the effectiveness and known risks of screening for prostate cancer" (2011, para 3). In fact, the article headline was "Prostate Cancer Screening May Do More Harm Than Good." Bawley cited the complex nature of cancer as well as acknowledging the good intentions of those who support screening. He referenced a consideration by the U.S. Preventive Services Force to advise *against* routine prostate screening, a move that actually came in 2012 (Simon 2012). The entire article could be quoted in support of the Awareness Equals Health Myth. For example, here is the core of Bawley's argument:

> Alas, the history of medicine is filled with examples of physicians jumping the gun, acting in a manner unsupported by evidence, even ignoring the words of caution in the "evidence-based guidelines" promulgated by their own professional societies.
>
> I am convinced that most advocates of screening and aggressive treatment are motivated by genuine desire to benefit men. Unfortunately, they are uninformed or unwilling to believe the reality that early detection and aggressive treatment of cancer is not always the best thing.
>
> For two decades, some supporters of prostate cancer screening, even some so-called experts, have overstated, exaggerated and, in some cases, misled the public about the evidence supporting its effectiveness. They downplayed or failed to mention the risks of screening and misapplied and misstated basic principles of cancer screening.
>
> With evangelical fervor, true believers conducted mass screening in shopping malls, at state fairs and in supermarket parking lots. Screening has been sponsored by medical practices, hospitals, drug and medical device companies, politicians and even manufacturers of adult diapers. Most of these sponsors wanted to do a public service, but many profited from it. Some may also have been blinded by that profit.
>
> The phenomenon of so-called experts, who do not understand basic principles of screening, making exaggerated statements is not limited to prostate cancer. It also occurs in breast and lung cancer screening. Well-designed scientific study has clearly showed that these procedures save lives, but science

has also demonstrated that the procedures have limitations and risks of harm (Bawley 2011, para 8-12).

In short, across multiple cancers, screening does save lives, but not without some risk of harm. Yet, as the *awareness culture* has built on the pink ribbon culture, the benefits of screening are trumpeted without reservation by organizations and sponsors such as the NFL and MLB while a deaf ear has largely been turned to any consideration of potential detriments. It is particularly daunting to write about Awareness Myths with the realization that for more than five years the American Cancer Society has cautioned about overemphasizing screenings, and yet the fundraisers and awareness months continue on behalf of screening.

It is worth noting, however, that Bawley's (2011) article did not include childhood cancers among those with exaggerated benefits of screening. The impact of the *awareness culture* is also at work here, in that while the possibility of some cancers, particularly breast, are sources of distorted fear (Orenstein 2013), there actually is a lack of awareness in terms of what Rogers (2003) would call how-to knowledge for some other cancers or diseases. In particular, childhood cancer, despite the success of campaigns such as the St. Jude "Give thanks. Give hope." campaign and the growing Go Gold movement in September, is not at the forefront of public consciousness.

Where Santos (2013) called awareness a "bullsh*t" word, a mother whose baby girl was diagnosed with cancer before her first birthday answered the question of what awareness means to her with the term "empowerment." She described searching symptoms on her phone in bed one night and "teratoma tumor" popping up. Because most cases were in third-world countries, she tried to put the alarming possibility out of her mind. She tried to believe the people who told her she was overreacting. "Childhood cancer awareness to me has nothing to do with checking yourself for lumps. It has nothing to do with raising money. I want to spread childhood cancer awareness to mothers and other caregivers. If you think something is wrong with your child, don't think you're crazy. . . . I want to spread childhood cancer awareness to empower mothers to not be afraid of being too cautious," she wrote.

"Not a day goes by that I don't wish I would have jumped out of bed when I saw teratoma tumor on my phone while I was Googling and rushed her to the ER and demanded an ultrasound. I have to know that I could have forced the doctors to find the tumor two months earlier than they did. That was two months that my baby (literally baby) was in pain and I could have found her relief sooner. Childhood cancer awareness to me is about empowerment to mothers and other caregivers."

Additionally, the mother of a son with incurable brain cancer discussed "the business of childhood cancer." Even though cancer is the leading cause of children's death by disease and two thousand children die each year from cancer, she said, the tax-funded National Cancer Institute defined childhood cancer as rare. "But by claiming childhood cancer is rare, despite its own statistics, the agency justifies granting less than four percent of total cancer funding to childhood cancer research," she added. She also learned how to "sniff out resources" and has committed herself to fundraisers that will "put money in the hand that holds the microscope."

As much as anything, the Awareness Equals Health Myth points out the ironies of the *awareness culture*. On one hand, breast cancer and increasingly prostate cancer are multi-million-dollar industries with the support of major, highly visible sponsors such as the NFL and MLB. On the other hand, childhood cancer, the second leading cause of death among children under the age of fifteen according to the American Childhood Cancer Organization, does not have the same level of visibility or fundraising prowess. For breast and prostate cancer screenings, the benefits have been overstated, while for childhood cancer—the growing Go Gold social media campaign in September not withstanding—the needs have been overlooked.

Awareness does not equal health, in part because health communication campaigns do not fully take lessons from theory and scholarship in providing evidence-backed information. In particular, awareness campaigns could provide helpful and beneficial information, use strategies that lead to a change in behavior, and *not* promote social norms of unhealthy behavior. Such an approach could improve health. And, perhaps save more lives.

Unit 3

Chapter Nine

The Awareness Myth Model

A goal in writing this book was to add our voices to those questioning the effectiveness of awareness health campaigns and to encourage communication scholars and professionals to move from awareness to prevention where possible and advocacy in all cases. We realize that the current *awareness culture* is so entrenched that a paradigm shift is not likely to arrive anytime soon. If anything, we are still in the "Magic Bullet" stage of awareness campaigns in which the idea is that if more people are aware, then things will automatically improve. The issue with the current state of health awareness campaigns, or more correctly observances, goes back to the Hippocratic Oath—First do no harm. While awareness seems innocuous, there is a growing body of evidence that awareness campaigns/observances actually *do* inflict harm by shifting attention and resources. As our previous chapters have covered, several myths are associated with awareness, and these myths are obstacles to effective prevention and behavior change campaigns. Furthermore, with the current *awareness culture* favoring causes and conditions that are the most visible or corporate friendly, some treatments and diseases are missing out on much needed and deserved funding.

A basic question communication professionals ask when designing communication campaigns is, "Is this a problem communication can solve?" We have considered that question at length and believe that communication can indeed help improve health and make lives better for those affected by conditions of health-related causes. First, scholars such as Backer, Rogers, and Sopory (1992) have cited successful health-related prevention and behavior change campaigns. There are also the noted benefits of reduced stigma. And, finally, we believe communication campaigns can address the obstacles of the *awareness culture* because communication campaigns helped create them.

Our research, primary and secondary, has led us to conceptualize the current state of *awareness culture* with the Awareness Myth Model. The Awareness Myth Model is based on observations, case studies, secondary research, autoethnography, and interviews. Through our study, a clear picture emerged of "awareness" as an all-encompassing, ever-growing bubble overriding and absorbing goals and objectives such as fundraising, education, treatment, cures, and research. Rather than awareness leading to increased action or specific goals, awareness itself was raised. Awareness was "raised" through shopping, events such as races and walks, and observances including awareness months complete with ribbons, of course. The strategies and tactics to raise awareness included types of amusement, even when outcomes were "actions" such as fundraising through events. Figure 9.1 demonstrates the Awareness Myth Model.

The Awareness Myth Model identified eight outcomes of awareness observances and campaigns. While on the surface some of these outcomes could be viewed as making an aware public into active public, to use Grunig and Hunt's (1984) model, our research indicated that the activity often functioned more to generate additional awareness than to lead to sustained action. For example, events and observances such as awareness months, races, walks, and rallies often had the purpose to raise awareness themselves. Likewise, donations to some organizations often are directed back to be used for additional awareness campaigns rather than research, screenings, or treatment. Research and treatment would also be an outcome many would point to as a positive outcome. We could largely agree, notwithstanding findings that some research and experts have questioned the appropriateness of the current approach to breast cancer and prostate screenings as well as treatments. Similarly, education contributed to the awareness cycle in that much of the awareness centered on statistics or promoting screenings rather than "how-to knowledge" for prevention or behavior change. Shopping and cause marketing put a commercial spin on the campaigns, and again were examples of buying something—which could be seen as an action—with the explicit goal of creating more awareness. For example, a consumer could buy pink gloves to raise awareness for breast cancer or purple socks to raise awareness for Alzheimer's. Social support from the awareness campaigns events is perhaps an outlier in that those affected by a condition can seek and provide support without intentionally engaging in additional awareness raising.

The Hierarchy of Effects of a Communication Campaign as presented by Backer, Rogers, and Sopory (1992) is useful in considering the current state of the *awareness culture* as depicted in the Awareness Myth Model. Backer, Rogers, and Sopory listed seven levels of effect:

(1) Audience *exposure* to message(s)

(2) Audience *awareness* of message(s)

(3) Audience's being *informed* by message

The Awareness Myth Model demonstrates the cycle of Awareness Culture, in which awareness campaigns are self-perpetuating. The "actions" from awareness campaigns often serve in fact to generate ever-increasing awareness rather than behavior change or sustained participation.

Figure 9.1. Awareness Myth Model Figure created by Hill and Hayes

(4) Audience's being *persuaded* by message
(5) Audience expression on *intent* to change behavior
(6) Actual *change* in audience's behavior
(7) *Maintenance* of audience behavior change (Backer, Rogers, and Sopory 1992, 7)

While evidence suggests that effects do not always occur in such a hierarchical fashion, the levels provide a framework for considering possible effects to campaign messages. In the current state of the *awareness culture,* the Awareness Myth Model demonstrates that there are no, or at least few, effects to be generated beyond "awareness." For example, the vast amount of messages found through our research were about "awareness" and not behavior change or maintenance. Additionally, Backer, Rogers, and Sopory (1992) addressed the adoption of an innovation through a health campaign, with an innovation categorized as an idea considered "new." It's possible if not likely that in the self-perpetuating Awareness Myth Model there is little true innovation to be adopted. Instead the information being disseminated has already reached a saturation point among those being exposed to the message.

Twenty-seven generalizations of successful health campaigns were identified by Backer, Rogers, and Sopory (1992). Five of those generalizations are especially relevant in the focus of moving beyond Awareness Myths to commitment. The first four generalizations, for example, can be taken individually but are best viewed as a unit:

> (1) More effective campaigns use multiple media (television, radio, print, and so on).
> (2) More effective campaigns combine mass media with community, small group, and individual activities, supported by an existing community structure (this involves using a "systems approach" to campaigns).
> (3) More effective campaigns carefully target or segment the audience that the campaign is intended to reach.
> (4) Celebrities can attract public attention to a campaign issue. Public attention can be achieved by embedding a campaign's message in an entertainment program. (Backer, Rogers, and Sopory 1992, 30)

We would concur with using multiple media and presume that a book written today would include the Internet in general and social media in particular. Additionally, our study supported the importance of the next two generalizations. In fact, we hold that a systems approach and careful targeting with messages and through multiple modes of communication are essential for successful communication efforts. In terms of generalization four, while we caution against amusement as a detrimental factor in the *awareness culture*, we also realize the potential of attracting attention through the use of celebrities. Our concern would be that the celebrity could take precedence over the cause.

We also highlight the final generalization: "(27) More effective campaigns use pretesting to ensure that campaign messages have the expected effects on target audiences" (Backer, Rogers, and Sopory 1992, 31). The endless loop of awareness observances, even with spotlighted months, detracts from setting and measuring objectives. In the next chapter, we address ways organizations can rewrite mission statements that can lead to improved measurement and thus potential for effective campaigns.

Going back to the Awareness Myth Model, the visualization of the model caused us to realize that awareness is being raised through the efforts of those most directly affected by the health-related cause. The websites, for example, seemed to be designed for those who were already aware. They provided platforms to shop, donate, or participate in events. Another problem with the Awareness Myth Model as currently exercised is that it focuses on the negative instead of the positive. As discussed previously, awareness can function to normalize behavior. Thus, while there is a belief that when people become aware of a problem they will do something to make it better, the opposite can actually happen. When people become aware that there is a problem, it can make them think that others are like them and the situation must not be so bad.

Perhaps the biggest breakdown of the Awareness Myth Model is that it is more susceptible to the Diffusion of Responsibility phenomenon than the Diffusion of Innovations communication paths. Darley and Latane (1968) studied Diffusion of Responsibility as well as the Bystander Effect and found through experiments that the more people who were aware of an incident, the less individuals felt responsible to act on it. In the case of health communication campaigns, this phenomenon turns awareness on its head. Rather than more awareness leading to more action, as has long been assumed, the Diffusion of Responsibility and Bystander Effect would predict that, ironically, the more people who are aware, the less likely any of them are to act.

The Diffusion of Innovations model (Rogers 2003) is still relevant for those implementing health campaigns and could actually be used to offset the Diffusion of Responsibility effect, but it must be used in concert with other communication principles—including those that are at odds with the current *awareness culture*. For example, the current *awareness culture* is all-encompassing without clear target audiences in many cases—after all, the assumption is that everyone needs to be aware. However, just as campaign models are seemingly built somewhat on the AIDA advertising model of Awareness/Attention, Interest, Desire, Action, there is another relevant advertising adage: "The everybody audience is the nobody audience." By taking such a broad approach, the awareness campaign/observances are missing the opportunity to target key publics with specific messages that could resonate. As the Diffusion of Innovations model would indicate, mass media are more effective at creating awareness, but persuasive messages are better suited to more personal channels.

Of course, the Diffusion of Innovations model and the Hierarchy of Effects of a Communication Campaign were developed before the advent of social media, which has added another element campaign planners must consider. Traditional communication paths for campaigns have often employed mass media, third-party intermediaries, and interpersonal communication. Rogers (2003) was among scholars who held that mass media was more appropriate for raising awareness and that, in fact, the effectiveness of communication could be hindered if awareness was first attempted through interpersonal means. Instead, an innovation would most likely be met with acceptance if it were introduced through mass media and then funneled through third-party intermediaries and finally discussed interpersonally, which was considered the most persuasive. Lionberger (1963) listed sources of information for stages in the adoption process. Mass media were most effective at the awareness and interest stages while friends and neighbors were most effective at the trial, evaluation, and adoption stages (Lionberger). For decades, the communication path models provided communication practitioners with a template for when and how to introduce campaigns—use campaigns to generate exposure and create aware publics and then through third-party intermediaries hopefully lead people to interpersonal communication that would persuade them to be active publics. Figure 9.2 depicts a traditional communication path model.

As noted previously, the Internet, which did not exist when traditional communication path models were developed, was a key factor we identified in the development of the *awareness culture*. Specifically as related to communication channels, the Internet in general and social media in particular can function as mass media, third-party intermediaries, *and* interpersonal communication. While we might question the linear, lockstep nature of the traditional communication path—instead seeing communication as evolving and cycling through loops rather than a straight line—we also recognize the contributions of the path in identifying how communication could flow through channels and with what effect. Our research did not specifically address the effects of communication channels, so we will not propose a new model but instead call for future research into how social media is and can be used to promote health-related causes and campaigns.

Traditional Communication Path

Mass Media ⟶ Third Party Intermediaries ⟶ Interpersonal Communication

In the traditional communication path model, information begins with mass media such as television or newspaper, going through credible third-party intermediaries and finally interpersonal communication. Mass media exposure is seen as being most effective at the awareness level while interpersonal communication is seen as more persuasive.

Figure 9.2. **Traditional Communication Path Figure created by Hill and Hayes**

As part of our methodology, which is posted at www.theawarenessmyth.com, we looked for "negative evidence" in our data that was not in complete agreement with our Awareness Myth findings. In other words, we were looking for examples of when awareness works or why people support awareness causes. We asked people what awareness means to them and why they support events and fundraisers for awareness campaigns. Two mothers of children with cancer provided powerful and poignant responses that explained why they organize and participate in awareness campaigns and fundraisers—including events, sharing information, and selling awareness products. The responses from these two mothers affected by childhood cancer were pivotal in helping us understand that within, or perhaps in spite of, the *awareness culture*, there are pockets of people engaging in activities beyond the hype to try to effect meaningful change and provide "how-to knowledge" that leads to sustained commitment rather than onetime participation. Their responses, included in full below, in part informed the Commitment-Communication Model presented in chapter 10.

AWARENESS AS EMPOWERMENT: A MOTHER'S STORY

BY MELODY HUBBELL

Being a mother is the most difficult job I have. You've probably read different blogs or Facebook posts about all of the hats mothers have on a daily basis. When you have a baby, you have one hat that you must wear at all times—mind reader. For a mother who has a healthy baby, she has to read their minds about when they are hungry, needs a diaper change, sleepy, happy, sad, scared and the list goes on. You know all of the signs for these. Mothers can tell a hungry cry from a sleepy cry. Mothers with babies who have tempers (yes, babies can get mad) know the tone of a mad cry. You learn what your baby needs based on signs like a cry. A routine also helps. It helps to know that it's time for a bottle. My oldest child pooped at the same time of the day. As they get older, they can articulate what they want and when they want it. Babies are difficult; they cannot talk. Mothers are mind readers.

Imagine being a mother and the cry your baby made was not the same cry as a hungry cry, a sleepy cry or mad cry. My little girl was saying, "I HAVE A MONSTER IN MY BELLY. MOMMY GET IT OUT!" and I could not read the signs. It was not like any of the cries I had ever heard. It was a cry from the pit of her stomach that was almost a screeching cry.

I put on my nurse hat and tried all of the tricks that I tried on my oldest child who was lactose intolerant and had severe reflux. He also had colic for 2 months. I had a list of tricks a mile long. I Pinterested and Googled every home remedy known to man. Nothing was working. One night I lay in bed and decided to get my phone out and google her symptom that was unlike anything I had ever seen: rectum hole stays open in infant. What I found was alarming. Teratoma tumor popped up. I read that most cases are in 3rd world countries and I had never heard of it. Because I was unaware of this type of tumor and it scared me, I shut my phone off and tried to go to sleep. I was UNAWARE. I forced myself to believe that that was not my daughter's problem. I spoke to people about Lucy and everyone assured me that I was probably overreacting. Had I been aware of the symptoms, I might have brought it to our pediatrician's attention. Had I not been afraid of being paranoid or being seen as a hypochondriac, I might have said something sooner. Had I known how many children have cancer, I might not have pushed a tumor out of my brain.

Childhood cancer awareness to me has nothing to do with checking yourself for lumps. It has nothing to do with raising money. I want to spread childhood cancer awareness to mothers and other caregivers. If you think something is wrong with your child, don't think you're crazy. Mothers' intuition is real. You know when your baby's cry is not the normal-every-day-cry. You know when your child is in pain from the inside out. I want to spread childhood cancer awareness to empower mothers to not be afraid of being too cautious.

Not a day goes by that I wish I would have jumped out of bed when I saw teratoma tumor on my phone while I was googling and rushed her to the ER and demanded an ultrasound. I have to know that I could have forced the doctors to find the tumor 2 months earlier than they did. That was 2 months that my baby (literally baby) was in pain and I could have found her relief sooner. No one can make me feel better about not taking childhood cancer seriously when I found it that night lying in bed. But, I can spread childhood cancer awareness so other parents won't wait like I did. They won't second guess anything and jump at the chance to be advocates for their children. Childhood cancer awareness to me is about empowerment to mothers and other caregivers.

THE HAND THAT HOLDS THE MICROSCOPE: ELI'S STORY

BY KRISTIE WILLIAMS

It was about 1 p.m. on an unseasonably warm December day, the second to last of 2011, when my third child, and oldest son, Eli, who just days earlier had turned seven years old, was at Huntsville Hospital having an emergency MRI of his brain. He had been having symptoms of nausea, fatigue, body pain, specifically in the back of his neck, since late September, but four visits to the pediatrician gained nothing except instructions to get him to the emergency room if his vision was ever affected. That morning, I caught him watching cartoons with one eye closed. "One of them goes away when I squint this eye," he explained to me. He was having double-vision. Knowing the wait would be long at the ER, I packed up some goldfish crackers, a water bottle, a couple of Hot Wheels cars, and watched him and his dad walk out the door.

I wouldn't see Eli again for several hours, and even then it wasn't when he came home, because he didn't. A couple of hours after Eli left, Vic, my husband and Eli's dad, called and put me on speaker between him and a doctor from the St. Jude Children's Research Hospital affilliate office. Eli was still in the MRI machine. She said that he had a "mass" on the back of his neck, so they were preparing an ambulance to take him immediately to the main St. Jude campus in Memphis, Tennessee. I sat down on the bed, right on top of the laundry I had been folding to busy myself while I waited . . . I thought I was waiting . . . for Vic and Eli to get home. Her voice slowed in my ear, the seconds passing as she talked became so heavy as I unsuccessfully tried to process what she was saying. Then the phone slid out of my hand down beside me on the bed, and the weight of the sky fell on our home.

The word "cancer" instead of "mass" wasn't used until about five days later, when the neurosurgeon at Le Bonheur Children's Hospital came to us to talk about the surgery and Eli's MRI scans. It wasn't until my own son had cancer that I epiphanized kids got cancer. To underscore that ignorance, a boy in our church had fought leukemia. But all I had comprehended was that he had been really sick, and was doing well. The End. That's how "aware" I was. I knew what pink stood for, and I knew that people who smoked for decades got lung cancer. But until it was in my house, I did not truly know it.

Eli's diagnosis of medulloblastoma, an aggressive childhood brain cancer that had metastasized throughout his brain and in his spine, set us on what cancer families call a "journey." A journey traveled with that weight of the sky on our shoulders. It has led us through deep valleys, to dark corners, along crumbling edges, and has even lifted us to fantastically high mountains from which the view can only be appreciated having traveled the journey below. This experience, in general, is the same for any cancer family, and is a bond that we all share. However, personalities, backgrounds, and responsibilities, the usual characteristics and influences that shape a person's attitude, drive, and interests, play a major role in how we each take on the challenge of cancer. I felt like my family had been attacked, therefore, my instinct, because of my personality, was to strike back. As a Christian, a Bible believer, I already knew our aggressor. Evil begets evil, so it is easily traced to its originator. I prayed that God take this evil being inflicted upon us, and turn it into good. That the nightmarish experiences be worth something, used in some productive way. I could think of no greater counter-attack than to turn Satan's own weapon against him.

Eli spent 10 months in Memphis undergoing a torturous treatment after that first diagnosis. The disease robbed him of a "normal" life, because the treatment ravages their little bodies. After surviving treatment, he was clear for 14 months. In December of 2013, the monster was back. This time, instead of the world's leading childhood cancer research center doctors handing me consent forms for the most innovative and promising treatment, I was sent home with paperwork for hospice care. There is no proven, sustainable, accepted treatment for relapsed medulloblastoma anywhere in the world. Statistically, Eli was given less than a five percent chance of surviving.

Over those two years, and the next, as we chased a relapse treatment that doesn't exist, I worked a lot on being "aware." I learned more and more about the business of childhood cancer. I learned that the National Cancer Institute, a tax-payer funded agency, claims childhood cancer is rare. Yet, in another sentence, the NCI said it is the leading cause of death by disease. According to the agency, six to seven children die from the disease every day, and 43 children are newly diagnosed every day. Being the number one killer of children by disease, and losing two thousand kids a year doesn't sound rare. But by claiming childhood cancer is rare, despite its own statistics, the agency justifies granting less than four percent of total cancer funding to childhood cancer research.

Was this it? Was this the reason my son and 2,000 others face death as children—money? Lack of money is the reason you stop eating out too much, or the reason you wear hand-me-down clothes, or the reason you rent instead of buy. But, in a country where wealth is abundant, and overflowing even in the most modest of homes, and advances in technology and science shame the rest of the world, there is no money. But, I learned that childhood cancer is simply not profitable. It only affects a small percentage of the entire population, so for-profit pharmaceutical companies will not spend billions of dollars developing a drug for a tiny percentage of the population because they can't sell enough of it to be worth the effort. Money. The reason I received rejection letters from doctor after doctor across the United States saying they did not have anything for Eli. The reason that I sat across from research doctors at two of the world's top five pediatric cancer research hospitals in 2015 after a second relapse to hear "We don't have anything. Take him home, and enjoy these days with him," is money. In describing myself earlier, I am slow to comprehension. I am oblivious to the obvious, but this became painfully clear that the key to new, innovative, and successful treatments is money!

When Eli relapsed the first time in 2013, a parent from another hospital—as opposed to our own doctor—suggested we try a palliative treatment to extend his life. Physically he was doing exceptionally well, and trials for new drugs might open up, so if the disease could be controlled with this mild treatment, he might enroll in something more curative. We took this advice. And, not only was the treatment a good choice for Eli, almost wiping out the disease, but it helped me to see beyond what was in front of us regarding treatment and research. It was like realizing a secret that nobody is able to just tell you. I learned more details about how and where research was conducted, the government's role in it all, and how to sniff out resources. Limited by my own intelligence, and comprehension skills, I at least knew now that there was more to it than just going to the closest hospital and taking the medicine the doctors there offered—or in our case didn't have to offer.

Three years into the fight, a seasoned, front-line soldier with a personality that desperately desired to fix, and to rescue, I felt a need to focus my attack with this revelation. I would never be a doctor or a nurse to participate in research, and we would never relocate for me to get a job at a research hospital to do whatever I could. Early on in this journey, we started having drives to raise money, or items to be donated to St. Jude, or the medical housing facilities. So, I had experienced the generosity of those touched by Eli's story already, and was overwhelmed by it. People wanted to do good, and they wanted to trust that their effort and money were going where they intended. Understanding now that funding is an issue for developing new treatments, and that so many of the mainstream non-profits give so little money to the actual cause they proclaim to support, I decided to focus my energy on subsidizing that four percent. Even if what I raised was small, I wanted to put money in the hand that holds the microscope. I decided to organize our own fundraising efforts as an official non-profit and seek out research labs testing innovative treatments for childhood cancers, specifically brain cancer. For me, for my personality, it satisfied two issues. It was the perfect strike against our aggressor in that people we meet would see our faith in action and look into learning from whom we gain our strength. Secondly, in all the chaos of cancer treatments, the chaos of being separated as a family, the chaos of our new "normal," it also helped me feel like I was part of the solution. Too many times I have sat across from doctors telling me there was nothing. Yet, each time, I have found someone, somewhere doing something. So, I wanted my effort to go toward changing that conversation in that little conference room between a doctor and a parent.

With only our energy and desire to do good, two friends, Jennifer Fortenberry, and Sharma Hamm, and my sister, Wendy Yeager, joined me in officially founding Eli's Block Party Childhood Cancer Foundation in January 2015. None of us had any non-profit experience, and we only had a $100 donation to get us started. By mid-year, Naomi Flanagan was added to the board, and Jerry Bryant came on in 2016. Our mission is to raise money to *donate to innovative research by hosting community events. My family has benefited overwhelmingly from the support of our community. I believe that we can raise awareness to the need for funding by creating these events that stimulate local tourism for our community. We also want to reach out to our local cancer families, and make sure they know they are not alone in what they face, and give them support where we can. Because Eli is a big car guy, we mostly host car shows to raise money. The plan is to extend our car show effort to other communities by partnering with car clubs, and individuals interested in our cause, bringing an Eli's Block Party to their town.*

In February of 2015, Eli's cancer was growing again, and by September 2015, after one failed trial, and one completed trial, he was given six weeks to live. He participated in another trial that also failed by January 2016, and was turned away from many trials because of his past treatment, and because the disease burden was so great. In March 2016, with his brain covered in 18 tumors, he was accepted into one of the most innovative immunotherapy trials open for kids—his fourth experimental trial. Nestled quietly in a south Georgia town at Augusta University, this one oncologist works tirelessly in his lab, and in his clinic to do more than treat cancer, but to fight it. Eli's cancer responded, and began to shrink again as of August 2016, one year from a six-week prognosis. It is efforts such as this that we want to sniff out and support as a foundation. As Eli continues to pioneer a path for kids yet to be diagnosed, our foundation is an encouraging distraction for me as the parent, a positive activity set against a very negative landscape. The time and energy that I pour into it is as much out of compassion for the victims, and a passion for the cause, as it is a vendetta against a killer.

Both of these accounts provide insights on the meaning of awareness. In the first account, note that the mother discussed spreading awareness of childhood cancer to other parents—those personally involved with the disease. The implication is that to get children the help they need, parents need to be the ones to do something about it. Therefore, parents need to trust their instincts and respond immediately if they think something is wrong with their child. The mother is not speaking to the general public and encouraging them to generally be aware of childhood cancer. She knows that parents are the ones to speak to and empower other parents. In the second account, the mother implies that spreading awareness is not the goal but instead she highlights the role of learning and a commitment to fighting the disease. In the next chapter, these points are incorporated into a new model that includes the role of personal relevance, knowledge, and other factors as people become committed to solving health problems.

Chapter Ten

The Development of the Commitment-Communication Model

In our previous chapters we have argued that awareness as an end point in public health campaigns is misguided and counterproductive. We discussed several myths of awareness: awareness is education, awareness is enough, awareness is acceptance, awareness is altruistic, and awareness is health. We depicted a model of how *awareness culture* currently operates, which is a cycle of ever-increasing awareness rather than behavior change or sustained participation that supports solving and alleviating health problems.

In this chapter, we propose the Commitment-Communication Model (Figure 10.1), which depicts three factors as affecting commitment to alleviating or solving a public health problem. Unlike previous models and theories of persuasion in public relations, our model is not linear or hierarchical. Instead, it is dynamic and processual. Entry can happen at any given point and movement can occur in any direction. Communication is the process by which all the variables interact.

In addition to public relations theory such as Situational Theory and Diffusion of Innovations, we draw from Bendinger's (2009) Think-Feel-Do Circle which depicts how people interact with products. In the Think-Feel-Do Circle, a person can enter into the model at any point and move throughout the process dynamically. For example, as Bendinger stated, a person can try a free sample (do), learn about it (think), and decide if he or she likes the product (feel), and then purchase the product or not based on his or her feelings. Alternatively, a person may have feelings about a product or brand (feel), then buy a product (do), then try a product and learn about it. There are many combinations using this model. We use the Think-Feel-Do Circle as an inspiration for how our model works. We will define the variables in the model and propose some relationships among them.

COMMITMENT

Commitment is the dependent variable in our model and refers to ongoing attempts to solve or alleviate a health problem and manage its deleterious effects. In advertising, the process of retaining customers is important (Bendinger 2009). Though purchasing products is not our focus, we wish to stress the importance of a long-term orientation to problem solving. Public health campaigns come and go but until diseases are eradicated and problems solved, there will be a need for people to stay engaged to reach this end. Commitment to addressing a problem will elicit (1) attempts to get others to recognize there is a problem and heightened sensitivity to messages about the problem, (2) ongoing attempts to seek information and become educated on the problem, and (3) participation in efforts to alleviate and solve problems. In order to effect change, people need an ongoing commitment to solving or

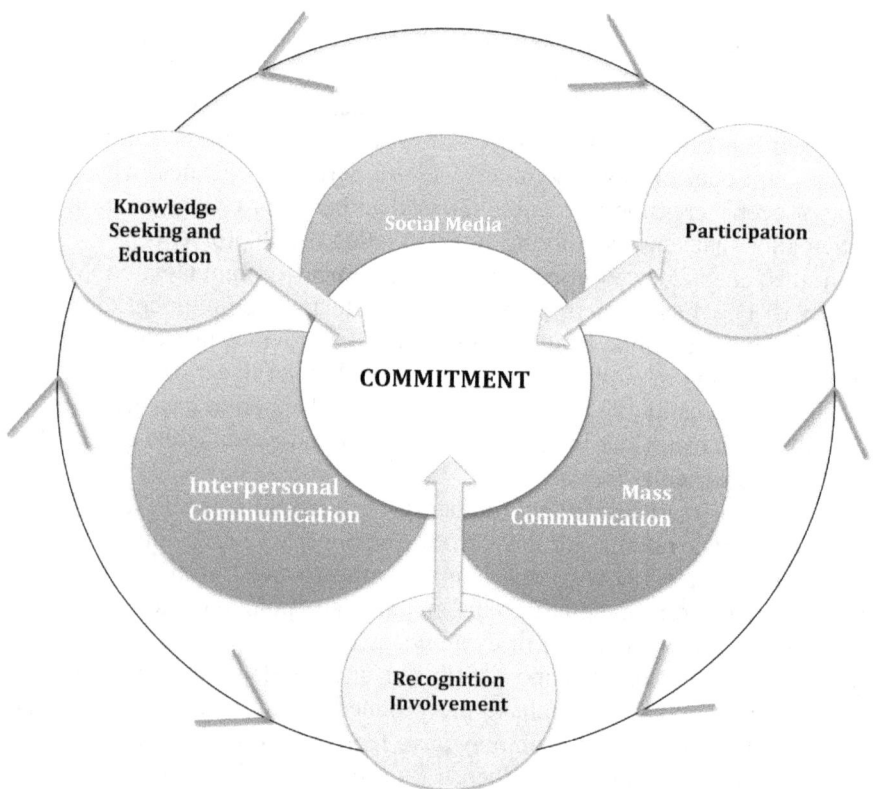

Figure 10.1. Commitment-Communication Model Figure created by Hill and Hayes

alleviating a problem. Attempts to get people involved who are not committed in awareness events may yield short-term results but little real change. The people who are likely to be the most committed to solving or alleviating a problem are people who experience personal salience and involvement with the problem. People who are not personally involved with a health problem may participate in efforts to solve the problem but these efforts are likely to be short-lived since those people are not invested in solving or alleviating the problem. The ultimate goal of any health campaign, regardless of the specific objectives, is to eradicate disease. Simply put, people need to be committed to solving health problems until they are solved.

RECOGNITION-INVOLVEMENT

Recognition-involvement refers to the degree to which individuals view a health problem as needing to be addressed and is based on perceived level of personal salience and involvement with the problem. People are exposed to and inundated with messages about health issues continually and must select which issues to attend to and address. Attempts to bring issues to light or capture the audience's attention will be unsuccessful or fleeting unless people feel that the issue is personally relevant and salient in some way. Uninvolved people may engage in passing events, such as clicking "like" on Facebook or even attending an awareness walk, but will not remain committed to solving or alleviating a health problem and will not effect much change.

Awareness is not featured in our proposed model but is reconceptualized and integrated into a new variable called recognition-involvement which draws from Grunig and Hunt's (1984) Situational Theory and Rogers's (2003) Diffusion of Innovations. In Situational Theory, "problem recognition" (e.g., when people recognize that there is a problem that needs to be addressed) is an independent variable that affects information seeking and processing. Another independent variable in Situational Theory that affects information seeking and processing is called "level of involvement" and refers to the extent to which people connect with the situation. Likewise, in Diffusion of Innovations, Rogers (2003) discussed not "awareness" in and of itself but instead discussed awareness-knowledge meaning that individuals must be exposed to an innovation and some basic knowledge about the innovation. Rogers further discussed the role of selective exposure in that people filter innovation messages based on their perceived need for the innovation. In other words, Rogers acknowledged that awareness-knowledge must become personally relevant to individuals for them to move through the innovation adoption process. Thus, our variable recognition-involvement bridges two ideas: cognizance of a problem that needs to be addressed, plus personal involvement as people are likely to filter out messages that are not personally relevant to themselves or to someone who is in their network.

Grunig and Hunt (1984) discussed groups of people called "publics" that can be classified according to their level of knowledge and involvement. Publics can be aware (high knowledge and low involvement), active (high involvement and high knowledge), inactive (low involvement and low knowledge), or aroused (high involvement and low knowledge). Active publics are the most likely to do something to solve a problem. They will seek information and act on that information. Thus, an active public is the ideal public and should be given top priority in accomplishing goals. We argue that people cannot be moved into being an active public without personal salience. It is only through personal salience that people will form an active public.

We are not stating that basic exposure to a health problem is entirely misplaced. We argue that for people to become committed to solving a problem, they must feel a problem is personally relevant. Andrew Solomon (2013) wrote in *Far from the Tree: Parents, Children, and the Search for Identity*, "Autism parents are activists. Not since the height of the AIDS crisis has there been such an aggressive campaign for funding and research" (222). It takes those affected by a disease or condition to be active.

KNOWLEDGE SEEKING AND EDUCATION

Knowledge seeking and education refers to the degree to which individuals seek knowledge about and become educated on a health problem. People who are affected by a health problem will seek to learn about it and how to manage it for themselves or others in their lives. They may seek knowledge through communication with health care providers, mass media messages, social media and technology, or other forms of communication, such as through formal and informal conversation about the health problem.

For example, if a person is diabetic, he or she may pay close attention to and seek out information on diabetes in order to understand and control the condition. Likewise, if a person has a close relationship with a person who has diabetes, he or she may seek out knowledge as well. A close friend of a diabetic may want basic knowledge of the disease as a basis for dining options, for example. People may actively seek information about the symptoms, causes, treatment, and possible cure for the disease through their own research on websites, talking to people living with the disease and condition, conversations with health professionals, support groups, etc.

People seek knowledge through communication channels such as mass media and interpersonal connections like friends, family, health care providers, and social media. Mass media have been the traditional channel used to reach audiences from a public relations perspective. According to Watson and Noble (2007), however, traditional channels are not the only way to communicate with stakeholders. The Internet is not only a tool to reach publics but is also a tool people can use to seek out knowledge and education, make participation decisions, and actually engage in activities to alleviate a problem.

In fact, it is inevitable that people affected by health problems will turn to the Internet and social media. Despite this inevitability, there are health care providers who caution people about using the Internet to seek health information. There are good reasons for such caution given that it can be difficult to judge the credibility of information on the Internet and some of the information is incorrect or contradictory. Still, according to Hesse et al. (2005) the results of survey data gathered in 2002 and 2003 by the Health Information National Trends Survey indicated that even at that time two-thirds of adults looked online for health information for themselves or someone else, with 40 percent of participants going online first. Those same respondents reported trusting their physician first, however. In fact, as Hesse and Moser (2010) indicated, trust in physicians may increase as people rely on their physicians to help them sort through information they learned about on the Internet. Recognizing the momentum and potential of the Internet and social media to affect health outcomes, several researchers have discussed how to use the Internet and social media to effectively improve health (Hesse et al. 2011; Korda and Itani 2013). Incorporating the Internet and social media into health campaigns and focusing on the role of the Internet and social media in research about health campaigns will continue.

PARTICIPATION

Participation refers to the degree to which people participate in specific activities, including communication activities, in order to solve or alleviate a health problem. We did a search on the Communication and Mass Media database using the search terms "participation health campaigns" and "participation awareness," but to date, we could not find published research that defines "participation" as we have. One study (Kiwanuka-Tondo, van den Berg, and Zuckerman 2003) examined the effects of outreach workers and audience members in campaign processes and goals in AIDS campaigns in Uganda. They found that audience participation can positively affect campaign message quality. However, this research simply focused on the effects of gaining input from campaign staff and audience members in order to construct more effective campaign messages. We also are interested in how people organically and actively organize and participate and how such participation interacts with other variables that lead to commitment through communication. Thus, although it may be of benefit for campaign planners to gain input from staff and audience members to construct messages, our focus is not unilateral and is one part of a dynamic process of commitment.

Our conceptualization of participation may include providing and receiving types of social support such as instrumental, information, or emotional support, whether face-to-face or in an online setting; donating to a cause; fundraising; etc. There are many ways to participate in alleviating or solving a health problem.

Individuals will monitor participation decisions as they actually implement the decisions and view the effects. If during actual participation, participation decisions appear to be fruitless or counter productive, individuals will make new decisions and participate in new ways. The cycle continues. For example, a person may attend a fundraiser with a specific group and then decide that the event was unproductive or that they simply did not like being a part of it. At this point, the person would find other events or activities to pursue.

There are cases where when people judge a health problem to be personally salient and relevant they may seek knowledge and education *as* they engage in participation activities. In this case, individuals learn as they go. For example, if a person is diagnosed with breast cancer, he or she may immediately join a support group or participate in a breast cancer walk and learn about the disease while being a participant. Participation and knowledge seeking and education are happening simultaneously in this case.

When people view their participation decisions as helping to solve or alleviate a health problem in some way, they are likely to continue them, although the degree to which they continue them will correlate with personal salience and an ongoing weighing up of participation decision options and assessment of their participation. People may alter their participation decisions and participation over time due to changes in knowledge, degree of personal salience, etc.

A person committed to solving or alleviating a health problem will not simply make a onetime participation effort but will engage in multiple ongoing participation activities. A person who is not committed may still attend events, etc., but again, will not engage in ongoing behavior to solve or alleviate a health problem. Perhaps one way to ascertain commitment is active membership in online social support communities since a person would have to have a motivation to sign up for such a site and participate in such groups.

COMMUNICATION

Communication refers to the modes by which messages are communicated such as mass media, social media, and interpersonal communication. As noted by Wright, Sparks, and O'Hair (2012) communication processes are "intertwined in complex and interesting ways" (1). The variables in our model are constructed through communication, and communication is the process by which movement occurs throughout the model and links the dependent variable, commitment, with the independent variables. Rogers (2003) discussed two communication channels, mass media and interpersonal communication. A recent public relations textbook (Lattimore et al. 2012) reiterated the ideas of Rogers and Lionberger. Lattimore et al. stated that there are five channels of influence: mass media, biased intermediaries, unbiased third parties, significant others, and personal experience. The textbook authors concluded that in the early stages of a campaign, mass media were most effective, while in the trial and evaluation stages, significant others were more important. In the adoption phase, the role of personal experience is most important. Social media has emerged as an additional channel of influence that warrants special attention as it may function in multiple ways to multiple effects.

For example, if an individual experiences symptoms such as fatigue, difficulty sleeping, or feeling "blue," he or she may wonder if he or she is depressed based on the knowledge of depression that has been accumulated through mass media, interpersonal relationships, etc. The individual may turn to the Internet to figure out what is wrong. After doing Internet research, he or she decides that he or she is more anxious than depressed, thus using knowledge seeking and education and problem recognition in a fluid fashion. So, he or she examines anxiety more closely, joins an online anxiety support group, and engages with it. He or she may engage in communication with health care professionals and even actively pursue specific courses of treatments that were learned about via social media. If a person comes to a point at which he or she no longer considers himself or herself to have a problem with anxiety and it has less personal salience, he or she may still engage in an online support group due to the relationships established and remain committed and continue to learn. A person may redefine how the health problem is conceptualized and view anxiety or what causes it and how it is experienced differently over time. The possibilities are endless.

An updated and current understanding of how communication channels function in a diffusion or adoption process is needed because the role of social media should be taken into account. It is interesting to note that in 2006, Noar, in a ten-year retrospective article on mass media health campaigns with directions for future research, gave scant attention to the role of social media and the Internet but focused almost exclusively on traditional mass communication channels. Future research on health campaigns would be wise to focus more on social media and the Internet. As stated by Korda and Itani (2013), although the Internet and social media provide opportunities to address an audience directly among other benefits, there is a need to study the effectiveness of various forms of social media in campaigns.

IMPLICATIONS FOR PUBLIC HEALTH CAMPAIGN PRACTICES

Foss (2016) provided eight steps for successful health campaigns that she drew from existing literature on health campaigns: (1) conduct audience analysis using focus groups, surveys etc., to define the target audience; (2) determine clear and realistic goals; (3) identify communication outlets to reach target audience such as websites, television, radio, etc.; (4) create an engaging campaign message within the social, economic, political, environmental, and cultural contexts; (5) pretest the campaign and make revisions; (6) conduct the campaign within a certain time frame; (7) evaluate the effectiveness of the campaign with qualitative and quantitative approaches such as surveys and focus groups; and (8) monitor the long-term effects of a campaign to maintain its effects. Foss's steps drawn from the health campaign literature offered a general format for the creation of health campaigns. We see our model as fitting within Foss's framework with several specific implications for practitioners.

(1) In terms of identifying a target audience, we emphasize the role of personal salience and involvement. Again, we assert that people are only active to the extent that a problem is personally salient. A sole focus on audience demographics will be limited if personal salience is not taken into account. Consistent with Watson and Noble (2007), communication and public relations experts need to focus more on listening to audiences. Likewise, health campaign organizers and planners could benefit from listening to audiences as well. One way this could be done is attending to social media groups and online communities that grapple with particular problems.

Although it may seem productive to reach people who are uninvolved, unware and uninformed, using different strategies may prove fruitless or simply not worth the effort (see Rawlins, 2006, for a review of public relations strategies and how they differ depending on characteristics of stakeholders and publics). There may be advantages to having specific messages designed to reach individuals that are not actively involved with the problem (i.e., latent, unaware, dormant groups, and so on), but starting with and focusing on an active group may bring tremendous power to a health campaign.

(2) In terms of determining clear and realistic goals, we argue that awareness should never be the goal of a health campaign. Current mission state-

ments in public health campaigns should be developed or rewritten so that awareness is not the ultimate goal of the campaign. For example, the Centers for Disease Control and Prevention (CDC) lists the following mission of the "Inside Knowledge: Get the Facts About Gynecological Cancer" campaign: "Raises awareness of the five main types of gynecologic cancer: cervical, ovarian, uterine, vaginal, and vulvar. When gynecologic cancers are found early, treatment is most effective." We believe the goal here is not truly "awareness" but rather is education. It is likely that people who have gynecological cancer already know much of this information. Thus, it is important to have a complex understanding of what people who have personal salience on this issue know and need to know. There are other such examples from the CDC. For example, the mission of the "Tips from Former Smokers" campaign is to raise "awareness of the negative health effects caused by smoking, and encourages smokers to quit and nonsmokers to protect themselves and their families from exposure to secondhand smoke." It is again likely that smokers know there are negative health effects of smoking. The idea of "Tips from Former Smokers" is a good one, but raising awareness of how bad smoking is for health in the mission statement does not seem productive. Yet another campaign is the "Let's Stop HIV Together" campaign. The mission of this campaign is again to raise "HIV awareness and anti-stigma campaign featuring individuals with HIV who share their personal stories along with their friends and family, and call on Americans to join the fight against HIV. The mission of the "Act Against AIDS" campaign is to "raise awareness about HIV and AIDS among all Americans and to reduce the risk of HIV infection among the hardest-hit populations—gay and bisexual men, African Americans, Latinos, and other communities at increased risk."

Furthermore, we recommend campaign planners understand and implement the distinction of objectives versus goals. Goals represent a long-term vision. As stated by du Pré (2013) the goal of health promotion campaigns is to influence people to engage in health-promoting behaviors. Health-promoting behaviors, as discussed by du Pré, are those that enhance health while reducing disease and risk. Given this definition, the goals of any campaign should fall into achieving this end. An objective, on the other hand, is a way to achieve a goal. The long-term goal of an HIV campaign is to prevent and eradicate HIV. An objective may be to increase the number of people being tested for HIV in a high-incidence population by a certain percentage within a certain amount of time. The goal of a stop-smoking campaign is to eradicate smoking. An objective would be to get a certain number of people enrolled in a stop-smoking program. Public health organizations should have a clearly articulated mission statement that encompasses the ultimate goals of a campaign and measurable objectives.

(3) In terms of identifying communication outlets, it is again important to note there is a shift away from traditional mass media outlets. Rogers (2003)

and Lionberger (1960) have discussed when certain channels are most appropriate. According to Neuhauser and Kreps (2003), health communication is most effective when interpersonal and mass media messages are combined. However, mass media messages are fragmented and easily filtered out. According to Hesse et al. (2005), there is a "tectonic shift in the ways in which patients consume health and medical information, with more patients looking for information online before talking with their physicians" (2618). Most people, however, consider their physicians to be the most trusted source of information and actually want their physicians to help them make sense of online data (Hesse, Moser, and Rutten 2010). Thus, it is likely that the modes of communication tend to work together.

Although there may be real and potential pitfalls in a reliance on the Internet for health information and participation, there must be a trend to provide accessible, credible information (Hesse et al., 2010). For example, "an easy-to-use Web portal leading the public to high-quality, secure, interactive sites would be a major contribution to what people say they want" (Neuhauser and Kreps 2003, 18). In addition to websites, people who have a health problem are often involved in online communities and support groups.

Reaching people via social media and technology seems logical and effective. It is important to tailor messages (Jensen et al. 2014) to people involved in social media groups and networks, but it is crucial to listen to people and observe their interactions in these groups as well. People who are involved in social media for health reasons are likely active and receptive to messages, but campaign planners have to know what the needs of these people are and how they function. Not only can health care campaign planners reach people via websites and social media, they can also understand their target audience better by researching these sites.

(4) In terms of creating engaging messages, it is important that the messages be specific. In order to truly educate or enhance knowledge of a disease or condition, choices have to be made as to what campaign planners want publics to know. For example, in order to truly educate the public about autism, health campaigns should focus on specific points rather than general "awareness." Health campaign planners should consider what they want the public to know about autism: that all people with autism are different, that it is a spectrum disorder, etc.

(5) It is important to monitor the pulse of public discourse beyond traditional ways of assessing campaign effectiveness. An insider's perspective of people who experience health issues must be taken into account. This perspective is likely to emerge from analysis of social media sites and communities, especially the interaction on such sites. Traditional surveys and focus groups can only go so far in understanding insider viewpoints and behaviors. As Miller-Day and Hecht (2013) stated, narratives are a promising avenue for health interventions. Such narratives can be identified via the Internet and

social media. In addition to revealing narratives, an examination of social media communities will allow researchers to observe *actual* interaction and behavior.

DIRECTIONS FOR FUTURE RESEARCH

The variables in our model, and the potential relationships among the variables, may prove heuristic for generating future research. We suggest a next step should be to conduct an interpretive study to understand the degree to which the variables and interactions among them comport with the lived experience of individuals. We are interested in studying factors that lead to and reinforce commitment. To this end, we recommend gathering a purposive sample of highly committed individuals and conduct in-depth, semi-structured interviews or focus groups to understand how highly committed people enact knowledge-seeking/education, recognition-involvement, and participation through communication.

In order to measure level of commitment, participants can initially self-identify as being highly committed to solving or alleviating a health problem and then answer a short questionnaire we have created to measure commitment. For the questionnaire, participants would first be asked to consider the health problem that they feel needs to be addressed. Then, they would be asked to respond to survey items using a Likert scale ranging from "strongly agree" to "strongly disagree." Example survey items to measure commitment are "I am dedicated to helping to solve or alleviate the health problem (I identified as needing to be addressed)," "I will not rest easy until the health problem (I identified as needing to be addressed) is solved or alleviated," "I feel an obligation to help solve or alleviate the health problem (I identified as needing to be addressed)," "It is my responsibility to solve the problem or alleviate the health problem (I identified as needing to be addressed)," and I have made a vow or promise to help solve or alleviate the problem (I identified as needing to be addressed)." Once a sample of highly committed individuals is recruited, they can be asked questions in order to confirm, extend, or modify how we have defined commitment as well as the rest of our variables. For example, they could be asked questions about how much time they spend seeking out information on the health problem, where they go to become educated on the problem, examples of when they learned more about the problem and how they learned it, etc. in order to understand knowledge seeking/education. In addition, participants can be asked how the problem is personally relevant to them and how involved they are with the problem in order to understand recognition-involvement more fully. Diagnosis stories may occur with such questions. Moreover, participants can be asked what activities they do to solve or alleviate the problem and the extent to which they think such activities are effective. Participations can further be asked about giving and receiving informational, instrumental, and/or emotional support and provide specific examples of those types of support. Participants can be asked about how they use social media and other types of communication as part of the process. Their use of social media is of particular interest. They can be asked if they are a member of any online social support groups, how they use social media, and how they think it helps or hurts the problem. They can be asked about recent conversations they have had about the problem and how those occurred and if their preference of certain modes of communication has changed over time. For example, maybe support groups were initially helpful but became less so as they learned more about the health problem. An excellent way to capture communication patterns would be to ask participants to keep a log of all their conversations that focus on the problem and note the type/content of conversation, the duration of conversation, and mode of conversation.

An interpretive study would thus allow us a greater understanding of the variables identified here and how they function and would allow us to build a survey, do a factor analysis of the survey, and test the relationships among them in a path model. We have already developed some survey items to measure commitment. We have some preliminary ideas for the other variables as well. For example, items to measure recognition-involvement could be "The health problem (I identified as needing to be addressed) is very relevant to me" and "(The health problem I identified as needing to be addressed) has a bearing on my life." Items to measure knowledge seeking could be "I seek out information on the health problem (I identified as needing to be addressed)" and "I educate myself on the health problem (I identified as needing to be addressed)." Additionally, items to measure participation could be "I take part in activities to solve or alleviate the problem (I identified as needing to be addressed)" and "I spend a lot of time engaged in activities to solve or alleviate the problem (I identified as needing to be addressed)." Measuring modes of communication may prove more difficult. Perhaps the best way to capture communication behavior may be to ask participants to keep a diary of all conversation pertaining to the health problem and record how long spent in conversation, the nature of conversation, and mode of conversation on the health problem participants identified as needing to be addressed. However, it is also possible to collect communication preferences for certain types of information more easily.

Based on our research thus far, we have created an initial survey to measure commitment as well as the other variables in the model. This initial attempt can be revised and built upon based on the results of our future interpretive study. Still we have made a contribution to the field of public health campaign research. We developed a process model in contrast to traditional hierarchical, linear models. The model we developed is an outcome of a line of research we have undertaken on health awareness campaigns. In our model, we decenter "awareness" and highlight the role of personal salience and participation, and emphasize the role of communication, especially social media, in explaining how people interact with health campaigns leading to commitment to solving and alleviating health problems.

We hope this research will prove heuristic and generate future research. We also hope that public health campaign practitioners will draw from the ideas and suggestions presented here for the betterment of public health campaigns. This book is our way of helping to eradicate health problems and alleviate suffering from a communication perspective, and we hope this first step will reverberate throughout the field of public health.

Bibliography

Aarthun, Sarah. 2010. "Revealing Facebook Posts Promote Cancer Awareness." *CNN*. Accessed January 8, 2016. http://www.cnn.com/2010/TECH/01/08/Facebook.bra.color/.

Abramson, Karley, Brian Keefe, and Wen-Ying Sylvia Chou. 2015. "Communicating about Cancer through Facebook: A Qualitative Analysis of a Breast Cancer Awareness page." *Journal of Health Communication* 20 (2): 237-243.

Altiere, Matthew J., and Silvia von Kluge. 2009. "Searching for Acceptance: Challenges Encountered while Raising a Child with autism." *Journal of Intellectual and Developmental Disability* 34 (2): 142-152.

Alzheimer's Association. http://www.alz.org/.

American Cancer Society. Accessed September 15, 2016. http://www.cancer.org/aboutus/whoweare/our-history.

American Childhood Cancer Organization. http://www.acco.org/childhood-cancer-awareness-month/.

American Heart Association. https://www.heart.org/HEARTORG/Research/Research_UCM_481866_SubHomePage.jsp

Aronowitz, Robert A. 2007. *Unnatural History: Breast Cancer and American Society*. New York: Cambridge University Press.

Backer, Thomas E., Everett Rogers, and Pradeep Sopory. 1992. *Designing Health Communication Campaigns: What Works?* Newbury Park, CA: Sage.

Bawley, Otis. 2011. "Prostate Cancer Screening May do More Harm than Good." *CNN*. November 1. Accessed September 1, 2016. http://www.cnn.com/2011/11/01/opinion/brawley-prostate-cancer-screening/ 2011.

Belkin, Lisa. 1996. "Charity Begins at . . . the Marketing Meeting, the Gala Event, the Product Tie-In." *New York Times Magazine*, December 22. Accessed October 20, 2015. http://www.nytimes.com/1996/12/22/magazine/charity-begins-at-the-marketing-meeting-the-gala-event-the-product-tie-in.html?pagewanted=allandpagewanted=print.

Belluz, Julia. 2014. "The Truth about the Ice Bucket Challenge: Viral Memes Shouldn't Dictate Our Charitable Giving." *Vox*, August 20. Accessed July 30, 2016. http://www.vox.com/2014/8/20/6040435/als-ice-bucket-challenge-and-why-we-give-to-charity-donate.

Bendinger, Bruce. 2009. *The Copy Workshop*. Chicago, IL: The Copy Workbook.

Bidwell, Allie. 2015. "Campus Sexual Assault: More Awareness Hasn't Solved Root Issues." *Newsweek*, May 20. Accessed August 5, 2016. http://www.usnews.com/news/articles/2015/05/20/sexual-assault-on-college-campuses-more-awareness-hasnt-solved-underlying-issues.

Breast Cancer Action. (2012). *Think Before You Pink Toolkit*. http://thinkbeforeyoupink.org/resources/think-before-you-pink-toolkit/.

Brown, Maury. 2015. "MLB sees record revenues for 2015, up $500 million and Approaching $9.5 billion." *Forbes*. https://www.forbes.com/sites/maurybrown/2015/12/04/mlb-sees-record-revenues-for-2015-up-500-million-and-approaching-9-5-billion/#188274d13e0e.

Buettner, Dan. 2015. "The Finnish Town That Went on a Diet." *Atlantic: Web Edition Articles (USA)*, April 7. *NewsBank*, EBSCO*host* (accessed October 9, 2016).

Centers for Disease Control and Prevention (CDC). Campaigns. Accessed July 1, 2016. http://www.cdc.gov/healthcommunication/campaigns/.

Cirino, Erica. 2016. "Health Awareness Months, Weeks, and Days." *Healthline*. Accessed September 26, 2016. http://www.healthline.com/health/directory-awareness-months.

Darley, John M., and Bibb Latane. 1968. "Bystander Intervention in Emergencies: Diffusion of Responsibility." *Journal of Personality and Social Psychology* 8 (4): 377.

Davidson, Jacob. 2014. "We Need to Do Better Than the Ice Bucket Challenge." *Time*. August 13. Accessed January 30, 2017. http://time.com/3107510/ice-bucket-challenge-als-we-need-to-do-better/.

DeFleur, Melvin, and Margaret H. DeFleur. 2016. *Mass Communication Theories: Explaining Origins, Processes, and Effects*. New York: Routledge.

Diamond, Dan. 2014. "The ALS Ice Bucket Challenge Has Raised $100 Million – And Counting." *Forbes*, August 29. Accessed February 20, 2016. http://www.forbes.com/sites/dandiamond/2014/08/29/the-als-ice-bucket-challenge-has-raised-100m-but-its-finally-cooling-off/#53a46deb5593.

Disabledworld.com. http://www.disabled-world.com/disability/awareness/ribbons.php.

Doyle, Barbara T. "Autism Spectrum Disorder: Myths and Facts." Johns Hopkins University School of Education. Accessed July 11, 2016, http://education.jhu.edu/PD/newhorizons/Exceptional%20Learners/Autism/Articles/Autism%20Spectrum%20Disorder%20Myths%20and%20Facts/index.html.

DuPre, Athena. 2013. *Communicating about Health: Current Issues and Perspectives*. New York, NY: Oxford University Press.

Evers, Kerry E., Janice M. Prochaska, James O. Prochaska, Mary-Margaret Driskell, Carol O. Cummins, and Wayne F. Velicer. 2003. "Strengths and Weaknesses of Health Behavior Change Programs on the Internet." *Journal of Health Psychology* 8 (1): 63-70.

Fawzy, Farida. 2016. "Ice Bucket Challenge's 2nd anniversary celebrates its gene discovery." *CNN*, July 27, 2016. Accessed August 5, 2016. http://www.cnn.com/2016/07/27/health/als-ice-bucket-challenge-funds-breakthrough/.

Foss, Katherine A. 2016. "Communicating Through Health Campaigns and Entertainment-Education." In *Storied Health and Illness: Communicating Personal, Cultural, and Political Complexities*, edited by Jill Yamasak, Patricia Geist-Martin, and Barbara Sharf (273-304). Long Grove, IL: Waveland Press.

Fowler, Jeremy. 2015. "DeAngelo Williams says NFL cited uniform policy in reasoning." *ESPN*. http://www.espn.com/nfl/story/_/id/13879055/deangelo-williams-pittsburgh-steelers-says-nfl-nixed-pink-plans-due-uniform-policy.

Green, Jesse. 1992. "The Year of the Ribbon." *New York Times*, May 3. Accessed October 9, 2016. http://www.nytimes.com/1992/05/03/style/the-year-of-the-ribbon.html?pagewanted=all.

Grunig, James E., and Todd Hunt. 1984. *Managing Public Relations*. New York: CBS College Publishing.

Hackley, Chris. 2005. *Advertising and Promotion: Communicating Brands*. Thousand Oaks, CA: Sage.

Hawkins, Robert P., Matthew Kreuter, Kenneth Resnicow, Martin Fishbein, and Arie Dijkstra. 2008. "Understanding Tailoring in Communicating about Health." *Health Education Research* 23 (3): 454-66.

Hesse, Bradford W., David E. Nelson, Gary L. Kreps, Robert T. Croyle, Neeraj K. Arora, Barbara K. Rimer, Kasisomayajula Viswanath. 2005. "Trust and Sources of Health Information." *Archives of Internal Medicine* 165 (22): 2618-2624.

Hesse, Bradford W., R. P. Moser, L. J. Rutten. 2010. "Surveys of Physicians and electronic health information." *NCBI*.

Hesse, Bradford W., Mary O'Connell, Erik M. Auguston, Wen-Ying Sylvia Chou, Abdul R. Shaikh, Lila J., Finney Rutten. 2011. "Realizing the Promise of Web 2.0: Engaging Community Intelligence." *Journal of Health Communication 16*: 10-31.

Hill, Myleea, and Marceline Hayes. 2014. "Is Awareness Bullsh*t? A Case-Study of Reactions to Childhood Cancer Awareness Month." Proceedings from the 17th annual International Public Relations Research Conference, Miami, Florida.

Hill, Myleea, and Marceline Hayes. 2015. "Do You Like It on the . . . ? A Case-Study of Reactions to a Facebook Campaign for Breast Cancer Awareness Month." *The Qualitative Report* 20 (11): 1747-1762.

Jacobsen, Grant D., and Katheryn H. Jacobsen. 2011. "Health Awareness Campaigns and Diagnosis Rates: Evidence from National Breast Cancer Awareness Month." *Journal of Health Economics* 30 (1): 55-61.

Jensen, Jakob D., Nick Carcioppolo, Andy J. King, Courtney L. Scherr, Christina L. Jones, and Jeff Niederdeppe. 2014. "The Cancer Information Overload (CIO) Scale: Establishing Predictive and Discriminant Validity." *Patient Education and Counseling* 94 (1): 90-96.

Jiwa, Bernadette. 2016. "Awareness is Overrated." *The Story of Telling*. Accessed January 30, 2017. http://thestoryoftelling.com/awareness-overrated/.

Kalb, Claudia. 2005. "Unlocking the Mystery of Autism." *Newsweek*, February 29.

King, Samantha. 2006. *Pink Ribbons, Inc.: Breast Cancer and the Politics of Philanthropy*. Minneapolis: University of Minnesota Press.

Kingsley, Emily P. "Welcome to Holland." *Child Autism Parent Cafe.com*. Accessed September 28, 2016. http://www.child-autism-parent-cafe.com/welcome-to-holland.html.

Centers for Disease Control and Prevention. Autism Spectrum Disorder. (ASD). Accessed September 27. https://www.cdc.gov/ncbddd/autism/index.html.

Kiwanuka-Tondo, James, Sjef van den Berg; and Cynthia Zuckerman. 2003. The Effect of Participation on the AIDS Communication Campaign Process in Uganda: An Organizational Perspective." Paper presented at the International Communication Association, San Diego, CA, 1-20.

Kolata, Gina. 2009. "Cancer Society, in Shift, Has Concerns on Screenings." *New York Times*, October 20. 2009. Accessed 20, 2016. http://www.nytimes.com/2009/10/21/health/21cancer.html?_r=0.

Kolata, Gina. 2015. "A Growing Disenchantment With October 'Pinkification." *New York Times*, October 30. Accessed September 20, 2016. https://www.nytimes.com/2015/10/31/health/breast-cancer-awareness-pink.html?_r=0.

Korda, Holly, and Zena Itani. 2013. "Harnessing Social Media for Health Promotion and Behavior Change." *Health Promotion Practice* 14 (1): 15-23.

Kreps, Gary L., and Linda Neuhauser. 2010. "New directions in eHealth communication: opportunities and challenges." *Patient Education and Counseling* 78 (3): 329-336.

Kristofferson, Kirk, Katherine White, and John Peloza. 2014. "The Nature of Slacktivism: How the Social Observability of an Initial Act of Token Support Affects Subsequent Prosocial Action." *Journal of Consumer Research* 40 (6): 1149-1166.

Lattimore, Dan, Otis Baskin, Suzette T. Heiman, Elizabeth L. Toth, and James K. Van Leuven. 2012. *Public Relations: The Profession and the Practice*. New York: McGraw-Hill.

Lavidge, Robert J., and Gary A. Steiner. 1961. "A model for predictive measurements of advertising effectiveness." *The Journal of Marketing*: 59-62.

Lionberger, Herbert F. 1963. "Individual Adoption Behavior, Applications from Diffusion Research–Part I." *Journal of Cooperative Extension* 1 (3): 157-66.

Lionberger, Herbert F. 1960. *Adoption of New Ideas and Practices*. Ames, IA: Iowa State University Press, p. 32.

Littlejohn, Stephen W., Karen A. Foss, and John G. Oetzel. 2017. *Theories of Human Communication*. Long Grove, IL: Waveland Press.

Mackay, Adrian. 2005. *The Practice of Advertising*, 5th ed. London: Routledge.

Maguire, John. 2014. "How Many People Donate after Ice Bucket Challenge?" *BBC*, September 12. Accessed August 5, 2016. http://www.bbc.com/news/uk-29170642.

McKeever, Brooke W. 2013. "From Awareness to Advocacy: Understanding Nonprofit Communication, Participation, and Support." *Journal of Public Relations* 25: 307-328.

Me, Merely. 2010. "Accepting Your Child's Diagnosis: Are We Going to Holland or Beirut?" *Health Central*. https://www.healthcentral.com/article/accepting-your-childs-diagnosis-are-we-going-to-holland-or-beirut.

Merriam-Webster Dictionary Online. 2016a. Aware. Accessed July 10, 2016. http://www.merriam-webster.com/dictionary/awareness.

Merriam-Webster Dictionary Online. 2016b. Knowledge. Accessed July 10, 2016. http://www.merriam-webster.com/dictionary/knowledge.

Merriam-Webster Dictionary Online. 2016c. Understanding. Accessed July 10, 2016. http://www.merriam-webster.com/dictionary/understanding.

Miller-Day, Michelle, and Michael L. Hecht. 2013. "Narrative Means to Preventative Ends: A Narrative Engagement Framework for Designing Prevention Interventions." *Health Communication* 28 (7): 657-670.

Moss, Danny, and Barbara DeSanto. 2011. *Public Relations: A Managerial Perspective*. Thousand Oaks, CA: Sage.

Muscarella, Anne. 2015. "The 19th Annual Webby Awards Honor the Internet's Greatest Trailblazers." *The Webby Awards*, May 18. Accessed August 5, 2016. http://webbyawards.com/press/press-releases/the-19th-annual-webby-awards-honor-the-internets-greatest-trailblazers/.

Nash, Madeline. 2002. "The Secrets of Autism." *Time*, May 6.

National Breast Cancer Foundation. Accessed June 30, 2016. http://www.nationalbreastcancer.org.

National Breast Cancer Organization. "Myths." Accessed July 12, 2016. http://www.nationalbreastcancer.org/breast-cancer-myths.

National Institute of Mental Health (NIMH). "Autism Spectrum Disorders." Accessed July 1, 2016. http://www.nimh.nih.gov/health/topics/autism-spectrum-disorders-asd/index.shtml.

National Association for Continence. http://www.nafc.org/conditions-2/.

Neuhauser, Linda, and Gary L. Kreps. 2003. "Rethinking Communication in the E-health Era." *Journal of Health Psychology* 8 (1): 7-23.

Niebur, Susan. 2010. "In the Name of Awareness." *The Toddler Planet*. Accessed January 30, 2017. http://toddlerplanet.wordpress.com/2010/01/08/in-the-name-of-awareness/.

Noar, Seth N. 2006. "A 10-Year Retrospective of Research in Health Mass Media Campaigns: Where Do We Go From Here? *Journal of Health Communication 11*: 21-42.

Nordrum, Amy. 2015. "Ice Bucket Challenge 2015: Can The ALS Association Turn Last Year's Viral Phenomenon into an Annual Fundraiser?" *International Business Times*, August 26. Accessed August 5, 2016. http://www.ibtimes.com/ice-bucket-challenge-2015-can-als-association-turn-last-years-viral-phenomenon-annual-2067736.

Orenstein, Peggy. 2013. "Our Feel-Good War on Breast Cancer." *New York Times*, April 25. Retrieved March 20, 2016, http://www.nytimes.com/2013/04/28/magazine/our-feel-good-war-on-breast-cancer.html?pagewanted=all.

Pennebaker, James W. 1997. "Writing about Emotional Experiences as a Therapeutic Process." *Psychological Science* 8 (3): 162-166.

Pezzullo, Phaedra C. 2003. "Resisting "National Breast Cancer Awareness Month": The Rhetoric of Counterpublics and their Cultural Performances." *Quarterly Journal of Speech* 89 (4): 345-365. DOI 10.1080/0033563032000160981.

Postman, Neil. 2006. *Amusing Ourselves to Death: Public Discourse in the Age of Show Business*. New York: Penguin Books.

Postman, Neil. 1985. *Amusing Ourselves to Death*. New York, NY. Viking Penguin.

Prevent Cancer Foundation. "Awareness Campaigns." Accessed September 27, 2016. http://preventcancer.org/our-work/programs/education/awareness-campaigns/.

Prostate Cancer Foundation. Accessed June 30, 2016. http://www.pcf.org.

Prostate Cancer Health Center. WebMD. Accessed September 26, 2016. http://www.webmd.com/prostate-cancer/prostate-cancer-myths-facts.

Rawlins, Brad. 2006. "Prioritizing Stakeholders for Public Relations." *Institute of Public Relations*. Accessed September 1, 2016. http://painepublishing.com/wpcontent/uploads/2014/03/prioritizing-stakeholders-Rawlins.pdf.

Rogers, Everette. 1962. *Diffusion of Innovations*. New York: Free Press.

Rogers, Everette, and Floyd F. Shoemaker. 1971. *Communication of Innovations: A Cross-cultural Approach*. New York: Free Press.
Rogers, Everette. 1982. *Diffusion of Innovations*. New York: Free Press.
Rogers, Everette. 1995. *Diffusion of Innovations*. New York: Free Press.
Rogers, Everette. 2003. *Diffusion of Innovations*. New York: The Free Press.
Rohrbach, Ben. 2015. "NFL fines DeAngelo Williams for raising breast cancer awareness during breast cancer awareness month." *Yahoo!Sports*. https://sports.yahoo.com/blogs/nfl-shutdown-corner/nfl-fines-deangelo-williams-for-raising-breast-cancer-awareness-during-breast-cancer-awareness-month-150703165.html.
Rothstein, Jeffrey D. 2014. "Five Myths about ALS." *Washington Post*, August 22. Accessed January 30, 2017. https://www.washingtonpost.com/opinions/five-myths-about-als/2014/08/22/70007ef2-2842-11e4-86ca6f03cbd15c1a_story.html?utm_term=.0c608adf6e5f.
Ryan, Bryce, and Neal Gross. 1943. "The Diffusion of Hybrid Seed Corn in Two Iowa Communities," *Rural Sociology* 8 (1): 15-24.
Rzucidlo, Susan. "Welcome to Beirut." *Beginners Guide to Autism*. Accessed September 30, 2016. http://www.bbbautism.com/beginners_beirut.htm.
Santos, Erin. 2013. "Awareness . . . What a Bullsh*t Word." *Huffington Post*. September 10. Retrieved October 9, 2016. http://www.huffingtonpost.com/erin-santos/awareness-what-a-bullshit-word_b_3867850.html.
Sifferlin, Alexandra. 2014. "Here's How the ALS Ice Bucket Challenge Actually Started." *Time*, August 18. Accessed March 10, 2016. http://time.com/3136507/als-ice-bucket-challenge-started/.
Simon, Stacy. 2012. "Task Force Recommends against Routine Prostate Cancer Screening." *American Cancer Society*. May 21. Retrieved September 1, 2016. http://www.cancer.org/cancer/news/task-force-recommends-against-routine-prostate-cancer-screenin.html/.
Singal, Jesse. 2014. "Awareness Is Overrated." *New York Magazine*, July 17. Retrieved September 20, 2016. http://nymag.com/scienceofus/2014/07/awareness-is-overrated.html.
Sinha, Smriti. 2014. "The NFL's Pink October Does Not Raise Money for Cancer Research." *VICE Sports*. https://sports.vice.com/en_us/article/the-nfls-pink-october-does-not-raise-money-for-cancer-research.
Solomon, Andrew. 2013. *Far from the Tree: Parents, Children, and the Search for Identity*. New York: Scribner.
Srivastava, Jatin, and Jennifer J. Moreland. 2012. "Diffusion of Innovations: Communication Evolution and Influences." *The Communication Review 15*, 394-312.
Strecher, Victor J., Brenda McEvoy DeVellis, Marshall H. Becker, and Irwin M. Rosenstock. 1986. "The Role of Self-Efficacy in Achieving Health Behavior Change." *Health Education and Behavior* 13 (1): 73-92.
Sulik, Gayle A. 2012. *Pink Ribbon Blues: How Breast Cancer Culture Undermines Women's Health*. Oxford, UK: Oxford University Press.
Surowiecki, James. 2016. "What Happened to the Ice Bucket Challenge?" *New Yorker*, July 25. Accessed August 10, 2016. http://www.newyorker.com/magazine/2016/07/25/als-and-the-ice-bucket-challenge.
The NonProfit Times. 2013. "10 Elements of an Awareness Campaign." June 25. Accessed June 16, 2016. http://www.thenonprofittimes.com/management-tips/10-elements-of-an-awareness-campaign.
This Is Diabetes. 2016. American Diabetes Association. http://main.diabetes.org/dorg/adm/adm-2016-fact-sheet.pdf.
United Nations Entity for Gender Equality and the Empowerment of Women. 2012. "Public Awareness and Education." Accessed September 27, 2016. http://www.endvawnow.org/en/articles/49-public-awareness-and-education.html?next=826.
U.S. Department of Health and Human Services. Accessed September 12, 2016. https://healthfinder.gov/nho/.
U.S. Department of Health and Human Services. National Heart, Lung, and Blood Institute. "Education and Awareness." Accessed September 27, 2016. http://www.nhlbi.nih.gov/health/educational.

U.S. Department of Health and Human Services. Accessed September 12, 5016. https://healthfinder.gov/nho/.
U.S. Department of Health and Human Services. https://healthfinder.gov/NHO/nho.aspx?year=2015.
Watson, Tom, and Paul Noble. 2007. *Evaluating Public Relations.* London: Kogan Page.
Webb, Thomas, Judith Joseph, Lucy Yardley, and Susan Michie. 2010. "Using the Internet to Promote Health Behavior Change: A Systematic Review and Meta-analysis of the Impact of Theoretical Basis, Use of Behavior Change Techniques, and Mode of Delivery on Efficacy." *Journal of Medical Internet Research* 12 (1): e4.
Wolff-Mann, Ethan. 2015. "Remember the Ice Bucket Challenge? Here's What Happened to the Money." *Money*, August 21. Accessed July 15, 2016. http://time.com/money/4000583/ice-bucket-challenge-money-donations/.
Wright, Jennifer. 2010. "You Don't Need Facebook to Raise Awareness about Breast Cancer." *The Gloss,* October 6. Accessed July 20, 2015. http://www.thegloss.com/beauty/you-dont-need-your-facebook-status-to-raise-awareness-about-breast-cancer/.
Wright, Kevin B., Lisa Sparks, and H. Dan O'Hair. 2012. *Health Communication in the 21st Century.* New York: John Wiley & Sons.

Index

ACCO, 33, 34, 35, 36, 41, 61, 79
AIDA, 47, 55
AIDS, x, xi, 3, 4, 14, 17, 18
ALS, 27, 37
Amusing ourselves to death, Postman, 25, 32, 49, 52
ASD, 46, 63, 64, 65, 66
Autism speaks, 27, 39, 40, 41, 79
Awareness is bullshit, 6, 54, 94
Awareness myth model, 11, 100, 102, 103
Awareness culture, 30, 32, 35, 36, 39, 41, 42, 53, 54, 55, 57, 61

Bendinger, 111, 112

Commitment model, 11, 14, 105, 111–112

DAGMAR, 47
Diffusion of Innovation, xi, 7, 8, 15, 16, 25, 29, 32, 41, 47, 49, 55, 103, 111, 113; Adopter categories, 8; Stages, 9, 10, 48, 103, 117
Diffusion of responsibility, 103

Facebook games, 6

Komen, xiv, xvn7, 13, 19, 20, 27, 74, 80

Levels of effect, 100

Magic Bullet Theory, 11
MLB, 31, 32, 75, 76, 94, 95

NBCAM, 14, 19, 28, 48, 49, 86
NFL, xvn6, 72, 73, 75, 76, 81, 94, 95, 99, 107

Obesity, 31, 89
Observances, 3, 4, 13, 14, 16, 18, 25, 41, 42, 45, 53, 55, 57, 60, 61, 62, 83, 84, 92, 99, 100, 102, 103

PCF, 31, 32, 41, 75, 76
Pinkification, 14, 50, 71, 73, 74, 84
Pink Ribbons, ix, x, xii, xvn1, 4, 13, 17, 19, 20, 21
Pinkwashing, xii, 78, 84, 86

Slactivism, 25
Social support, xi, xiv, 14, 20, 41, 57, 67, 100, 116, 121
Sociological Placebo, xvii, 62, 83
Situational Theory, 111, 113; Publics, 7, 35, 41, 55, 114

Year of the ribbon, 4, 14, 16, 17

About the Authors

Myleea Dawn Hill (EdD, 2005, Arkansas State University) is a professor of strategic communication in the Department of Communication at Arkansas State University. Hill is the author of several manuscripts on social media, communication education, and journalism. Her work appears in journals such as *Communication Teacher* and in edited volumes such as *Social Media and Strategic Communication*. Hill, a former reporter and photographer, has done consulting work with over a dozen local and regional organizations in the areas of photography, writing, and website design. Her awareness research agenda can be found at www.theawarenessmyth.com.

Marceline Thompson-Hayes (PhD, 2000, The University of Memphis) is a professor of communication studies and chair of the Department of Communication at Arkansas State University. Hayes is the author of several published manuscripts on computer-mediated communication, relational communication, and qualitative research methods. Her work appears in journals such as *Journal of Family Communication*, *Computers and Human Behavior*, and *Argumentation and Advocacy*. Her awareness research agenda can be found at www.theawarenessmyth.com.

ABOUT THE FOREWORD AUTHORS

Susan Jacobson (PhD, New York University) is assistant professor of Journalism + Media, Florida International University. Jacobson has worked in new media across her professional and academic career. Her research is concerned with how social media shapes the relationship between journalists and news audiences, the impact of new media on journalism, and the expressive qualities of multimedia. Her work has been published in top-ranked journals such as *Information, Communication and Society*; *New Media and Society*; and *Journal of Broadcasting and Electronic Media*. She has won fellowships and awards from Mellon Foundation, the Media Ecology Association, and the Warburg Institute. She is a breast cancer survivor interested in how social media may help breast cancer patients.

Lynne M. Webb (PhD, University of Oregon) is professor of communication, Florida International University. Her research examines interpersonal communication in a variety of forms, venues, and relationships. Webb has coedited three scholarly readers and published over eighty essays including multiple theories, research reports, methodological pieces, and pedagogical essays. Her work has appeared in numerous national and international journals including the *Journal of Applied Communication, Health Communication,* and the *International Journal of Social Research and Methodology* as well as in prestigious edited volumes including *Handbook of Family Communication* (Sage, 2014) and *Handbook of Research on the Societal Impact of Digital Media* (IGI Global, 2015). She is the 2015 recipient of the Osborn Teacher-Scholar Award, the Southern States Communication Association's highest award; in 2012, the University of Arkansas designated her a Fulbright Master Researcher.

www.ingramcontent.com/pod-product-compliance
Lightning Source LLC
Chambersburg PA
CBHW052051300426
44117CB00012B/2066